CULTURE SMART!
LIBYA

Roger Jones

·K·U·P·E·R·A·R·D·

ISBN 978 1 85733 453 1

British Library Cataloguing in Publication Data
A CIP catalogue entry for this book is available from the British Library

Copyright © 2008 Kuperard
Second printing 2010

First published in Great Britain 2008
by Kuperard, an imprint of Bravo Ltd
59 Hutton Grove, London N12 8DS
Tel: +44 (0) 20 8446 2440   Fax: +44 (0) 20 8446 2441
www.culturesmart.co.uk
Inquiries: sales@kuperard.co.uk

Distributed in the United States and Canada
by Random House Distribution Services
1745 Broadway, New York, NY 10019
Tel: +1 (212) 572-2844 Fax: +1 (212) 572-4961
Inquiries: csorders@randomhouse.com

Series Editor Geoffrey Chesler
Design Bobby Birchall

Printed in Malaysia

About the Author

ROGER JONES is an English lecturer and writer specializing in careers, living and working abroad, and classical music. After graduating in modern languages from King's College, London University, he worked in education for extended periods in several different countries, including Libya. He has written fifteen specialist handbooks on planning to live and work abroad and is the author of *Culture Smart! Thailand* in this series. He is a member of the Career Writers' Association and the Society of Authors and was formerly a member of the Chartered Institute of Management and the Institute of Administrative Management.

The Culture Smart! series is continuing to expand.
For further information and latest titles visit
www.culturesmartguides.com

The publishers would like to thank **CultureSmart!**Consulting for its help in researching and developing the concept for this series.

CultureSmart!Consulting creates tailor-made seminars and consultancy programs to meet a wide range of corporate, public-sector, and individual needs. Whether delivering courses on multicultural team building in the USA, preparing Chinese engineers for a posting in Europe, training call-center staff in India, or raising the awareness of police forces to the needs of diverse ethnic communities, it provides essential, practical, and powerful skills worldwide to an increasingly international workforce.

For details, visit www.culturesmartconsulting.com

CultureSmart!Consulting and **CultureSmart!** guides have both contributed to and featured regularly in the weekly travel program "Fast Track" on BBC World TV.

contents

contents

Map of Libya

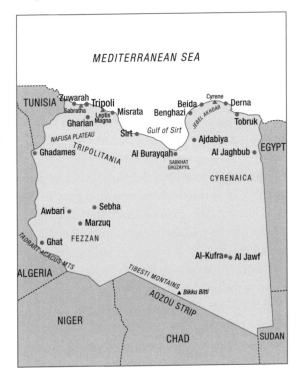

introduction

What does Libya mean to you? To historians and archaeologists it is home to some of the most spectacular Greek and Roman ruins in the world. For soldiers it was a famous battleground in the Second World War where Allied armies fought against the might of Rommel's Afrika Korps. To statesmen and political observers it has long been a rogue state that has aided and abetted revolutionary and terrorist movements.

After years in comparative isolation Libya is opening up again. Its relations with the rest of the world have now improved, and with the lifting of sanctions it is likely that more outsiders will have a chance to visit it both for business and for pleasure. The time therefore seems ripe to reassess the country and its people.

In 1950 this Arab country situated on the southern shore of the Mediterranean was one of the poorest nations on earth, and with its three distinct regions (Tripolitania, Cyrenaica, and the Fezzan) was far from being a unified entity. Everything changed when oil was discovered, and Libya has never looked back.

To many the country and its people are an enigma. It is an Arab country unlike other Arab countries. It is an African country, but it doesn't feel like Africa. For the uninitiated, the Libyans are difficult to fathom. But their values and attitudes have been shaped by their past and traditions, many of which date back centuries. Libyan territory has been occupied by Carthage, Rome, Arabia, Morocco, Egypt, Spain, the Ottoman Empire, and Italy. That is why some appreciation of its history is essential in order to understand the sensibilities of Libyans today.

This slim volume aims to offer an insight into the Libyan people and their view of life. Such information will enhance your stay in their country and ensure that you do not commit too many faux pas. There are chapters on customs and traditions, and the rapidly changing nature of modern Libyan life, with advice on what to expect and how to behave appropriately in different situations. For the business traveler there is guidance on how to deal with government structures and policies, and how to make the most of the opportunities that present themselves.

Above all, *Culture Smart! Libya* should help you to become acquainted with a nation of resilient, outgoing, and friendly people who, when they greet you with the words "*ahlan wa sahlan*," are completely genuine in their welcome.

Key Facts

Official Name	Great Socialist People's Libyan Arab Jamahiriya (which means State of the Masses) / Al Jamahiriya al Arabiya al Libiya ash Shabiya al Ishtirakiya al Uzma	
Head of State	Muammar Qadhafi	Official titles: Brother Leader of the Revolution and Supreme Commander of the Armed Forces
Capital City	Tripoli (pop. approx.1 million)	
Major Cities	Benghazi, Misrata, Beida,Sebha, Derna, Sirt	
Population	Approx. 6 million; population growth 2.5%	The Libyan workforce is approx. 1.8 million.
Area	686,000 sq. miles (1.76 million sq. km)	
Ethnic Makeup	Arab and Berber 97%. Others 3% (incl. Greeks, Maltese, Italians, Egyptians, Pakistanis, Turks and Tunisians)	
Age Structure	0–14, 33.6% 15–64, 62.2% 65 plus, 4.2%	
Life Expectancy	Male – 74.46 yrs Female – 79.02 yrs	
Geography	Borders Egypt, Sudan, Chad, Niger, Algeria, Tunisia, and Mediterranean Sea.	The longest land border is with Egypt: 600 miles (1,115 km)

Terrain	Largely desert with fertile coastal strip	Jebel Akhdar mts. in the east; Tibetsi mts. in the south. Nafusa plateau in the northwest
Climate	Mediterranean with mild winters and warm summers in coastal areas. Dry desert climate inland	A hot, dry wind from the Sahara, the Ghibli, blows in spring and fall.
Language	Arabic, with three main dialects: Tripolitanian, Southern Libyan, and Eastern Libyan	Other languages: English, Italian, French
Literacy Rate	80% of adults	
Religion	Sunni Muslim (97%) Other (3%)	
Currency	Libyan dinar. Issued in 10LD, 5LD, 1LD, 500 dirham and 250 dirham notes	
GDP	US $75 billion (2006 est.)	
Media	State controlled radio, TV, and newspapers, and one privately owned broadcaster	The main daily newspapers are *Al-Fajr Al-Jadeed*, *Al-Jamahiriya*, *Al-Shames*, and *Az-Zahf Al-Akhdar*.
Electricity	220/240 volts, 50 Hz	Mainly two-prong sockets
Telephone	Libya's country code is 218.	To dial out of Libya, dial 00 and the country code.
Time Zone	GMT +2 hours	

LAND & PEOPLE

GEOGRAPHY

Libya is the fourth-largest country in Africa and the second largest (after Algeria) in North Africa. With an area of 679,400 sq. miles (1.76 million sq. km) it is larger than Alaska and its neighbor Egypt yet its population numbers only some six million. To the north is the Mediterranean Sea, to the west it is bounded by Tunisia and Algeria, to the east Egypt and to the south Niger, Chad, and Sudan.

Most of the country (90 percent) is covered by desert with oases dotted here and there. Ninety-five percent of the population lives close to the coast,

especially the Al Jifarah plain in the western part of Libya, which includes the country's capital, Tripoli. There are no permanent rivers, but riverbeds (*wadis*) can flood after heavy downpours of rain.

The country is fairly flat with the exception of the Nafusa plateau south of Tripoli, the Jebel Akhdar (Green Mountain) region east of Benghazi, and the Tibesti mountain range in the south of the country. The lowest point in Libya is Sabkhat Ghuzayyil, a lake 164 ft (47 m) below sea level, and the highest point Bikku Bitti in the Tibesti mountain range near the border with Chad, which is 7,930 ft (2,267 m) above.

The Libyan Flag

The Libyan flag is just one color—green—symbolizing devotion to Islam. Its adoption in 1977, however, could also have a connection with Qadhafi's *Green Book*, which details his political aims, including the transforming of Libya into a wealthy, green agricultural nation.

The Regions of Libya

Libya did not become a unified political entity until the twentieth century. Before that it was three distinct regions—Tripolitania, Cyrenaica, and the Fezzan—separated from one another by vast tracts of desert. Each retained its separate identity until the 1960s, with the Gulf of Sirt marking the divide between not only the two regions bordering the Mediterranean but also the western Arab world (Maghreb) and the eastern Arab world (Masriq).

Tripolitania forms the northwestern part of the country. The Greeks named its three cities—Sabratha, Oea (present-day Tripoli), and Leptis Magna—Tripolis, which became Regio Tripolitania under the Romans. Tripoli's cultural ties are with the other Maghreb countries, Tunisia in particular, and its importance was derived from its position as a terminal for the trans-Saharan trade routes. As a result of these contacts Tripolitanians are often perceived as more cosmopolitan in outlook than other Libyans.

Cyrenaica is the eastern region and takes its name from Cyrene, the first Greek settlement in the area. Historically this part of Libya has always had close links with Egypt. Because of its relative isolation over the centuries it has been relatively untouched by outside influences. Cyrenaicans tend to be rather more conservative than other Libyans and, while hospitable by nature, are sometimes distrustful of strangers.

The Fezzan, for much of its history, has been populated by nomads plying the trade routes between the oases. Its main connections have been with sub-Saharan Africa and the Mediterranean coast. The Fezzanis are desert people who are resourceful and no strangers to hardship.

CLIMATE AND SEASONS

The populated areas along the Mediterranean coast enjoy a Mediterranean climate, which means mild winters and warm summers. Sometimes the temperature can go as high as 95°F (35°C). Tripolitania suffers, in the spring especially, from a wind called the Ghibli that blows from the Sahara bringing with it a lot of sand, and in the desert dust storms and sandstorms are common. The hilly areas, especially the Jebel Akhdar in Cyrenaica, are generally cooler. Annual rainfall, which tends to be intermittent, is around 15 inches (40 cm) a year near the coast.

There is a greater range of temperature in the desert areas of the interior, where at night the temperature can drop below freezing. In summer temperatures can reach 120°F (50°C), but during the rest of the year daytime temperatures higher than the upper 70s F (25°C) are rare.

THE PEOPLE

It is not clear who were the original inhabitants of the area we now know as Libya. We do know, however, that by the time the Phoenicians arrived in the first millennium BCE the country was already populated by Berbers, whose ancestors are believed to have migrated there from southwestern Asia in the third millennium BCE. Berbers refer to themselves as *Imazighen* (free men) and their languages, not always mutually intelligible, belong to the Afro-Asiatic language family.

During the time of the Pharaohs many Berbers served in the Egyptian army, and some rose to high positions. After the invasion of the Bedouin Arab tribes in the seventh century CE most became assimilated by their conquerors, though not completely. There are small pockets of Berber speakers in places such as Gharian in the hills south of Tripoli and in some desert oases, while in the desert regions you will come across Tuareg tribes who speak a Berber language called Tamazight.

In addition to the native Libyans, there are large numbers of immigrant workers who have flooded in from neighboring Arab countries as well as from Africa south of the Sahara and give the major cities a cosmopolitan feel. Estimates (which are far from reliable) range from a few hundred thousand to as many as two million. There is additionally a much smaller number of Westerners involved mainly in commerce, education, and the oil business. Even during the period of sanctions Western staff were employed at Libya's oil installations.

Libya used to have a Jewish community— one of the oldest in the world. In the late 1940s there were still 38,000 Jews, many of whom emigrated to the newly formed state of Israel. Around 7,000 remained until 1967, when the Six-Day War between Egypt and Israel led to anti-Jewish riots. The last Jewish resident of Libya died in 2002.

There was also a large Italian community, which settled here in the 1930s. But since independence and particularly since the post-Revolution property confiscations the number of Italians has dwindled.

Libya and Libyans Defined

For most of its history the words Libya and Libyan have meant a number of different things. The name Levu (Libyan) was first used by the Ancient Egyptians in the third millennium BCE to designate one of the Berber tribes carrying out raids into Egypt. The Ancient Greeks applied the name Libya to most of North Africa and to the Berbers who lived there. During the reign of Diocletian (284–305 CE) the Romans used the names Upper and Lower Libya (Libya Superior and Libya Inferior) for their two provinces in Cyrenaica. The name Libya was revived when the Italians annexed the territory in the twentieth century.

A BRIEF HISTORY
Phoenicians and Greeks
Our first knowledge of Libya comes from Phoenician traders from what is now Lebanon, who set up trading posts along the North African coast including Oea (now Tripoli), Labdah (Leptis Magna), and Sabratha around the first millennium BCE. They developed commercial ties with the Berber tribes, notably the Garamantes, who controlled many of the trans-Saharan trade routes.

These settlements later came under the control of the Phoenician state of Carthage. Founded near to present-day Tunis in c. 614 BCE, Carthage was to become the dominant sea power in the Western Mediterranean, until displaced by Rome.

The eastern coastline attracted Greek settlers from the island of Thira (present-day Santorini), who established a colony at Cyrene in 635 CE. Its prosperity was derived from the cultivation of silphium, a medicinal plant that cured coughs, chest complaints, and snakebite. Four other Greek cities were established in the area: Barce, Euhesperides (present-day Benghazi), Teuchira, and Apollonia. Together they made up the Pentapolis (Five Cities).

Although the Greeks of these cities were able to resist attack from the Carthaginians and Egyptians, they were no match for the Persians, who overran the region in 525 BCE. Alexander the Great entered Cyrenaica in 331 BCE and on his death it was ruled by the Ptolemy dynasty. During this time Cyrene became one of the leading intellectual and artistic centers of the Greek world.

The Roman Period

Carthage eventually came into conflict with the rising power of Rome, which waged three wars (the Punic Wars) and finally achieved the total destruction of Carthage in 146 BCE. Tripolitania came under the control of the Berber king of Numidia, but under Julius Caesar it became a

Roman province (Regio Tripolitania). In 96 BCE
Ptolemy had bequeathed Cyrenaica to Rome
and it was joined to Crete for a while during the
reign of the Emperor Augustus. Rome
conquered the Garamantes in the south and
named the region Phazania.

Despite coming under Roman control the
Punic language and culture lingered on in
Tripolitania until the sixth century—Punic was
a later form of Phoenician, influenced
by Berber languages—and Greek
traditions persisted for a while in
Cyrenaica. The Roman period was
a time of relative prosperity,
certainly in Tripolitania, but less so
in Cyrenaica. A number of the Jews
had been deported from Jerusalem to
Cyrenaica after their abortive rebellion against
Roman rule in 70 CE and they felt strongly
antagonistic to Rome. In 115 CE a Jewish revolt
in Cyrenaica spread through Egypt to Palestine,
causing tremendous destruction and loss of life,
including the sack of Cyrene.

One of the most significant figures of the
period was Septimius Severus, who was born in
Leptis Magna in 146 and rose to become Roman
Emperor in 193 CE. He died in 211 CE during a
campaign to subdue those parts of Britain not
yet under Roman rule. He arranged for many

embellishments to his native city, which
became the capital of Diocletian's new province
of Tripolitania toward the end of the third
century CE. Tripolitania was assigned to Rome's
Western Empire, while Cyrenaica, now
designated Libya Superior
(or Pentapolis) with a
capital at Ptolomais, and
Libya Inferior (Sicca) with
Paraetonium as its capital,
both became part of the
Eastern Empire.

Christianity spread from
Egypt in the third century.
One of the most prominent
Cyrenaicans of this period
was the philosopher
Synesius, who was made
bishop of Ptolomais in 410 CE.

In the early fifth century the Vandals captured
much of North Africa, including Tripolitania,
and made Carthage their capital. They launched
raids on Italy, sacking Rome in 455, but their
success was short-lived. The Byzantine general
Belisarius took back North Africa for Rome but
control did not extend much beyond the coast,
and the area drifted into decline and decay. The
same was true of Cyrenaica, which remained an
outpost of Rome's Eastern Empire.

The Arab Conquest

The conquest by the Arabs was one of the most significant events in Libyan history. In 642 CE, ten years after the death of the Prophet Mohammed, Arab armies commanded by Amr ibn al-As moved first into Egypt and then Cyrenaica. They sacked Leptis and Sabratha, and took Tripoli in 643. They later moved into the province of Africa (Ifriqiya) and founded the city of Kairouan in what is now Tunisia.

However, resistance by the Byzantine garrisons along the coast of Tripolitania as well as by the Berber inhabitants meant that it was not until well into the eighth century that the Arabs consolidated their hold on the region.

The Arab conquerors became an urban elite, but many intermarried with Berber women. The Berber tribes in the hinterland may have remained hostile to the Arabs, but they readily embraced the Islamic faith, adapting it to their own tastes. The Kharijite doctrine, with its democratic but puritanical outlook and emphasis on the literal interpretation of the Qur'an, proved particularly attractive to them.

In the following centuries Tripolitania came under the control of various Arab and Berber dynasties, notably the Aghlabids, Fatimids, and Hafsids, but for most of the time it languished as a backwater.

In Cyrenaica, after the demise of the Fatimids, the Mamluk dynasties of Egypt exercised nominal control over the territory in the eleventh and twelfth centuries. However, de facto control was in the hands of Bedouin tribal leaders, who demanded protection money from pilgrims and caravans traveling between the Maghreb and Egypt.

In the Fezzan, Bani Khattab chieftains held sway, like the Garamantes of old, until displaced in the sixteenth century by a Moroccan adventurer named Mohammed al Fazi, whose successors remained undisputed rulers of the region under Ottoman suzerainty.

The Ottoman Period

In 1510 the forces of King Ferdinand of Spain captured Tripoli, destroyed it, and constructed a fortified naval base there. In 1524 it was placed under the protection of the Knights of St. John in Malta.

Spain's great rivals in the Mediterranean were the Ottoman Turks, who were beginning to establish colonies along the North African coast.

In 1551 the Turkish admiral Sinan Pasha wrested control of Tripoli from the Knights of Malta and a Turkish pirate captain, Draghut Pasha, was installed as governor. Although Draghut was successful in establishing control of the coastal areas, he was far less so with the nomads of the interior, and his influence did not extend to Cyrenaica and the Fezzan. Tripolitania had very few resources of its own at this time and one of the main sources of income came from piracy along what became known as the Barbary Coast.

The Karamanli Dynasty

Following a period of military anarchy in Tripolitania, a popular cavalry officer, Ahmad Bey Karamanli, seized control of Tripoli, assassinated the governor, and bought the title Pasha-Regent from the Sultan with property confiscated from Turkish officials he had assassinated.

He asserted Tripoli's autonomy from Istanbul, turning Tripolitania into an independent kingdom, established diplomatic relations with European countries, increased revenues from piracy, won allegiance from the Bedouin and Berber tribes, and by the time of his death in 1745 had extended his authority to Cyrenaica and the Fezzan.

He and his descendants presided over prosperous times and developed trade with other countries, especially Malta and Italy. Shipowners paid protection money for the free passage of their ships in that part of the Mediterranean. However, the American government refused to pay such forms of tribute and this led to a conflict between the USA and Tripoli that lasted from 1801 to 1805. President Jefferson despatched warships to the Mediterranean and there was a particularly ugly international incident when the American frigate, the *Philadelphia*, was captured off Tripoli and sunk in Tripoli harbor.

Rule by the Karamanlis lasted until 1835, when dispute over the succession and appeals for assistance to put down a rebellion enabled the Ottomans to regain power and eject the Karamanli dynasty.

The Second Ottoman Period

Under the Ottomans Tripolitania, Cyrenaica, and Fezzan became the Turkish province (or *vilayet*) of Tripolitania under a governor-general (*wali*) appointed by the Sultan. In 1879 Cyrenaica was separated from the rest of the province and its lieutenant-governor reported directly to Istanbul.

The most significant development of the nineteenth century took place in Cyrenaica with the establishment of an Islamic order or brotherhood near to the city of Cyrene. Founded by Sayyid Mohammed Ali al-Sanusi, the movement spread through the province and into the Fezzan. Supporters of the Sanusiya offered support to the Ottoman regime and thereby helped to counter the spread of French influence from the south.

Eventually, Sayyid Mohammed moved the headquarters of the Sanusiya order to the oasis of Jaghbub near the Egyptian border, and later it was moved further south to Al-Kufra.

Libya Under Italian Rule
The Italian Invasion

In 1911 the Italians, aware that the Ottoman Empire was in steep decline, seized the chance to declare war and, on September 28, invade Libyan territory with an expeditionary force of 35,000. The Italians supported the landings in Tripoli,

Benghazi, Derna, and Tobruk with aircraft that dispatched bombs, making these the first air raids in history.

Turkish troops led by Enver Pasha and Mustafa Kemal (later to become known as Ataturk) enlisted the help of Arab tribes to resist the invasion, but with war threatening in the Balkans the Sultan sued for peace with Italy. However, the 1912 peace treaty was ambiguous, and the Ottomans did not relinquish sovereignty over Tripoli, even though they withdrew their troops from Libya.

The Italians encountered stiff resistance in the interior from Sanusiya units led by Ahmad ash-Sharif, especially in Cyrenaica, and eventually they were forced to withdraw.

Ahmad was pressured by the Ottomans to support a campaign against the British in Egypt led by Turkish officers. This was put down by British forces, and Ahmad surrendered leadership of the Sanusiya order to Idris, whom Britain and Italy recognized as the Amir (ruler) of the interior of Cyrenaica.

After the end of the First World War the victorious Allies accepted Italy's sovereignty over Libya and limited political rights were granted to people in areas under occupation. The Italians confirmed Idris as Amir of

Cyrenaica, granting him autonomy over much of the interior of that province and also providing him with a subsidy.

In 1918 a group of nationalists led by Ramadan al-Suwayhli, an Egyptian by birth, proclaimed a Tripolitanian Republic and called on Italy to recognize it. The Italians at the time considered coming to terms with them, but there was considerable dissension among the various Libyan factions and they were unable to present a united front. The situation changed with the appointment of the strong-minded Count Giuseppe Volpi as governor, who advocated a policy of military pacification.

The Tripolitanian nationalists then offered to recognize Idris as Amir of Tripolitania, believing this to be a way of advancing independence. At first Idris declined the offer as he was not anxious to extend his political or his religious influence to Tripolitania, and he also recognized that neither he nor the Sanusiya order could command much loyalty there. But after some consideration he accepted the proposal. He then fled to Egypt to avoid capture by the Italians.

The Cyrenaican Resistance

By now Mussolini had come to power, and in 1923 Italy occupied Sanusiya territory near Benghazi. But while northern Tripolitania was

quickly brought under Italian control, followed by the rest of Tripolitania and the Fezzan over the next few years, the Cyrenaicans were not prepared to surrender without a struggle. Led by Sheikh Omar Mukhtar, the Sanusiya forces, numbering a few thousand, waged a guerilla war against the Italians. The Italian General Graziani brutally put down all forms of dissent. It is estimated that half a million Libyans died in the conflict.

Omar Mukhtar: Lion of the Desert

The exploits of Omar Mukhtar and his soldiers were immortalized in an epic film released in 1981 with Anthony Quinn in the title role, Rod Steiger as Mussolini, Oliver Reed as General Graziani, and a cast of thousands. Directed by Moustapha Akkad with music composed by Maurice Jarre, it was shot in the desert 600 miles (960 km) from Benghazi and cost $35 million to make. However, it recouped only $1 million at the box office, making it a contender for the biggest financial disaster in movie history. The film was financed by Muammar Qadhafi.

Eventually the Italians' superior technology and manpower won through and in 1931 the Italians attacked Kufra, the last stronghold of the Sanusiya. The resistance collapsed and its leader, Omar Mukhtar, was hanged before a crowd of 20,000 Arabs. The Italians then proceeded to destroy all the Sanusiya lodges (*zawias*).

The Italians Consolidate Their Power

In 1934 the Italians molded their North African colony into a single entity, which they named Libya. Administered by a governor-general, it consisted of four provinces: Tripoli, Misrata, Benghazi, and Derna; the Fezzan remained under separate military control. In 1939 Libya became a part of metropolitan Italy.

The 1930s were a period of considerable change with a great deal of investment in the country's infrastructure. Cities were modernized, port facilities extended, a railway built, and in 1937 a coastal highway, 1,100 miles (1,800 km) in length, was completed between the Tunisian and Egyptian borders.

Land owned by Libyans was confiscated and given to settlers from Italy under Mussolini's "economic colonization" scheme. The first 20,000 settlers arrived in 1938 and by 1940 there were 110,000 of them living in Libya, about 12 percent of the population. A state

corporation known as the Libyan Colonization
Society was established that reclaimed land and
built model villages for the settlers. Meanwhile,
little was done to improve the lot of the
indigenous population.

The Second World War
When war broke out in 1939 Libyan political
leaders met in Alexandria and accepted Idris as
leader of the nationalist cause. In 1940 Fascist
Italy invaded Egypt, then under British control,
and the Cyrenaicans declared their support for
the Allies. The Tripolitanians eventually came
on board, albeit with some reluctance. Britain
welcomed Idris's support and pledged that the
Sanusiya would never again fall under Italian
domination. With the help of five Libyan
battalions, recruited largely from the ranks of
former Sanusiya resistance fighters, British
troops managed to expel the Italians, later
replaced by German forces who pushed the
British back to the Egyptian frontier. The
Desert War between Rommel's Afrika
Korps and the Allied Eighth Army
commanded by Field Marshal
Montgomery raged for the
next few years until Rommel's
army was routed and forced
back as far as Tunis.

The Aftermath of the Second World War
At the end of the war Italy was forced to relinquish sovereignty over Libya. Separate British military administrations were established for Tripolitania and Cyrenaica, while the French controlled the Fezzan.

The USA, the Soviet Union, Britain, and France then had to make decisions as to the future of these three territories. One plan suggested the creation of three trusteeships to be administered by Britain, France, and Italy respectively. Many Libyans, however, favored unification of the three provinces and, when the matter was referred to the United Nations, it was decided that the final decision should rest with representatives drawn from all three provinces. When they came out in support of unification the UN General Assembly supported them and in 1949 passed a resolution to grant Libya independence not later than the beginning of 1952.

The representatives agreed that the Amir of Cyrenaica should be their ruler, and so on December 24, 1951, King Idris Sanusi proclaimed the establishment of the United Kingdom of Libya.

Independent Libya
The Monarchy 1951–1969
Sayyid Idris al-Sanusi, the first ruler of the now independent United Kingdom of Libya, ascended the throne at the age of sixty-one. A descendant of

the Grand Sanusi who had founded the Sanusiya brotherhood in Cyrenaica, he had become leader of the Sanusiya and Amir of Cyrenaica (or, rather, parts of it) in 1916.

During the Italian occupation Idris had gone into exile in Egypt where he remained until the British occupation of Libya in 1942. He returned permanently to Libya in 1947 to head a government in Cyrenaica supported by local tribesmen.

Idris was an ascetic, scholarly, self-effacing person, who has been dubbed "the reluctant king." He, as well as some of his supporters, would have been perfectly content for him to remain just the Amir of Cyrenaica rather than become the ruler of three very disparate territories.

The newly independent state faced many challenges. It was one of the poorest countries in the world with a per capita income of around US $25 a year. Its main revenue came from the export of castor seeds, esparto grass, and scrap metal left over from the Desert War. Libya's population was around one million in 1951, most of the people living at subsistence level and in rural areas. Three-quarters lived in Tripolitania, where much of the fertile land was in the hands of around 50,000 Italian settlers. The infant mortality rate was 40 percent, and

94 percent of the population was illiterate. Only 34,000 young people were receiving any education, and there were just twenty-five Libyan secondary school teachers and fourteen Libyans with degrees.

Libya's economy received a boost when the government signed agreements with Britain and the USA to allow them military bases on Libyan soil and by the end of 1959 the country had received more than $100 million in aid from the USA. But that year the country's fortunes began to look up.

The discovery of oil was to change Libya forever. Over the next decade it would become the fourth-largest oil producer in the world, and the government managed its negotiations with the oil companies with considerable skill to extract maximum advantage from them.

During the 1960s the country changed from a loose federation into a unitary state with more powers accruing to the King and the central government. There was a big influx of people from the country into the towns, and increasing numbers of Libyans started benefiting from an education that had been denied to their elders.

However, politically the country remained moribund. The government was in the hands of the King's close supporters, his own family, tribal leaders from Cyrenaica, influential families, and business leaders. Although the King professed to favor political reform, he lacked the energy and boldness to put it into effect for fear of alienating his core supporters.

The population—notably the young, the urban middle class, and lower ranking army officers—grew increasingly disenchanted. Tripolitanians, who represented the majority of the population, were not impressed when Idris decided to locate Libya's new capital at Beida, in the Sanusiya's heartland, to the east of Benghazi.

In addition Libyans were exposed to President Nasser's relentless propaganda from Radio Cairo, which chided Libya for its close affiliations with the West and urged Libyans to embrace the concept of Pan-Arab socialism. During the Six-Day War of 1967, in which Egyptian forces were humiliated by the Israeli Army, anti-Western riots broke out in Tripoli and Benghazi.

The monarchy was becoming increasingly remote from the aspirations of its citizens, but it limped along for another two years. Out of deference to public opinion, negotiations started with the Americans and British regarding the closure of their bases in Libya.

Opinions about the Idris regime are mixed. On the one hand, it was something of an anachronism that failed either to unify the country or equip it with the trappings of a modern state. On the other, it was a relatively benign regime that had made considerable social, economic, and educational progress from unpromising beginnings.

The Al-Fateh Revolution

On September 1, 1969, Libyans awoke to find that a group of junior army officers and enlisted men had staged a coup d'état and taken control of all government installations. The leader of the coup was a twenty-seven-year-old captain, Muammar Qadhafi, who broadcast the news from the radio station in Benghazi.

The coup caught nearly everybody unawares. Originally, Qadhafi and his followers had planned to stage it in March of that year, but the authorities got wind that something was up and cracked down on possible subversion.

Initially there were pockets of resistance to the coup in Tripoli, but most of the populace quickly accepted the new regime. King Idris, who was on holiday in Ankara at the time, abdicated, and the revolution was virtually bloodless. He went to live in Egypt, where he was to die in 1983 aged ninety-four.

The astonishing fact about the coup was that it had been carried out by no more than five hundred junior army officers and servicemen. Despite the distances involved and the need for secrecy, it had been masterminded to take place simultaneously in the capitals of all three regions. That the coup succeeded probably had more to do with the incompetence of the regime than any desire for political change among the population at large.

Most people knew nothing about the officer who would be named the commander-in-chief of the new regime. Since he would dominate Libyan politics in the decades ahead the time is opportune to become better acquainted with Muammar Qadhafi.

The Qadhafi Phenomenon

Some leaders are born with a silver spoon in their mouths, but this was definitely not the case with Qadhafi. He was born in 1942 in a tent near Abu-Hadi, 50 miles (80 km) south of Sirt, the only surviving son among five children. His parents were Bedouin and belonged to a small tribe of Arabized Berbers called the Qadhafa.

His was a simple life with hardly any exposure to the mass media. But he would have been aware of what was happening around him from the stories he heard from his father and grandfather, who had both fought against the Italians and who regarded Europeans with profound suspicion.

His father had a herd of goats and camels and led an itinerant life. As a result the young Muammar's education was intermittent and informal. He was taught initially by a peripatetic teacher, known as a *fatih*, and did not start his regular education until 1954 when he was eleven. However, he proved to be a diligent pupil.

He began his secondary education in Sebha in the Fezzan in 1961, but was expelled after organizing a demonstration in support of Arab unity following the breakup of the United Arab Republic of Egypt and Syria. He continued his studies at Misrata, during which time he began to print and distribute political pamphlets.

His education was deeply rooted in Islam and he grew up a devout Muslim espousing an austere code of personal conduct and morals. He set great store by family ties, personal honor, and social egalitarianism, and he regarded urban politicians with considerable distrust.

Qadhafi decided to join the army—much against his family's wishes. However, it was a sensible choice for an ambitious young man, since it was one of the few paths to advancement for those like himself coming from humble backgrounds. Besides, he was constantly reminded of the success of the Egyptian army and Gamal Abdel Nasser in taking over the government of that country and modernizing it.

Nasser was clearly an inspiration to him when he entered the Military Academy at Benghazi, where he became deeply enmeshed in politics and set about organizing an underground military grouping that was to become the Free Officers' Movement. Qadhafi graduated in 1963 and was one of a group of Libyans selected to attend a signals course in England. It would appear that on the first course at Beaconsfield the Libyan soldiers did not take to the rough and ready manner of British military life and relationships between them and their lecturers and other trainees were strained. This son of the desert hated London, but developed a liking for the English countryside.

On his return he enrolled as a history student at the University of Libya and continued with his political activities. He gathered around him a number of junior officers who had similar backgrounds to him and shared his views. He was particularly outraged when the Idris government stood idly by as Israel inflicted defeat on Egypt in the Six-Day War.

Four factors, in particular, provide the key to Qadhafi's outlook on life and indirectly to the policies he was later to pursue: the Pan-Arabism of President Nasser of Egypt, the painful experience of Italian colonialism, the tribal culture he grew up in, and Islam.

Revolutionary Government

It was not until a week after the coup that Libyans discovered the identity of their new leader and it was only at the beginning of 1970 that they learned the names of the Revolutionary Command Council who would take the Revolution forward. All the RCC members had belonged to the Free Officers' Movement and were contemporaries of Qadhafi. None held any rank above that of major; none had any political or economic expertise.

But their determination to bring about radical change was not in doubt. Britain and the USA were given notice to close their bases and withdraw their troops; foreign banks, insurance companies, and hospitals were nationalized; Italians were informed that their properties would be confiscated; much of the oil industry came under state control; officers above the rank of major were dismissed and the army doubled in size; high-ranking bureaucrats and supporters of the monarchy were removed.

Qadhafi sought to combat political apathy by establishing Popular Congresses to elect parliamentary representatives and a president. But this idea was quickly abandoned in favor of the creation of the Arab Socialist Union (on the Egyptian model), and laws were passed banning any political activity outside the ASU, which would be punishable by death.

However, the ASU's progress did not satisfy Qadhafi, who criticized the Libyans' lack of revolutionary fervor, and in 1973 he proclaimed a Cultural Revolution. This involved:

- the annulment of all laws made by the previous regime and their replacement by *sharia* law
- the repression of communism and conservatism (those opposed to the Revolution)
- equipping people with arms in order to protect the Revolution
- the reform of the bureaucracy
- the promotion of Islam

To put these policies into effect people's committees were set up.

Five years after the Revolution chaos and confusion reigned. The bureaucracy had more than doubled in size and replacing seasoned administrators with inexperienced ones had made it dreadfully inefficient. Tensions mounted within the ranks of the RCC over whether or not to pursue a more technocratic approach to Libya's problems and there was considerable student unrest.

In August 1975 two members of the RCC attempted a coup, which proved abortive. The RCC was now reduced to five members and Qadhafi consolidated his position by purging the army and ministries of all elements he suspected of potential disloyalty. He also began to place members of his own family and tribe in sensitive positions in the army.

Buoyed up by increasing oil revenues he became ever bolder in his political ambitions. In 1976 he disappeared into the desert to formulate his political theories in *The Green Book*, a slim publication that set out the blueprint for the prospective Libyan state, which he designated the Third Universal Theory.

Qadhafi advocated statelessness, a political system in which people would manage their own affairs without state institutions. He put this theory into effect in 1977 when Libya was proclaimed a *Jamahiriya* (State of the Masses). Private property was eliminated, private trading abolished, state supermarkets took over all retail activities, Libya's embassies abroad were renamed People's Bureaus.

During this time he challenged the role of the *ulama* (Islamic jurists and scholars) as interpreters of Islam and sought to reinterpret the Qur'an in the light of modern conditions and needs. His attack on the traditional religious establishment was relentless and he seized mosques, replacing their *imams* (prayer leaders) with others more compliant to his ideas. The remaining RCC members were dismissed, and Qadhafi took over nearly all policy decisions, which he channeled through the General People's Committee (the quasi-cabinet) to give the appearance of legitimacy. By surrounding himself with a small coterie of loyalists his regime was starting to look very similar to the regime he had overthrown.

The Third Universal Theory

Qadhafi began to promote this theory (also known as the Third International Theory and Third Theory) in the early 1970s. It is a synthesis of his ideas on Arab unity, independence, economic egalitarianism, and cultural authenticity, and represents an alternative ideology to capitalism and communism.

It rejects the class exploitation of capitalism and the class warfare and atheism of communism in favor of a system that eliminates class differences and embodies the Islamic principle of consultation with all citizens in both community and national affairs. Central to the theory are the concepts of religion and nationalism as embodied in Islam, which Qadhafi holds to have been the "two para-mount drives that have moved forward the evolutionary process." He advocates "positive neutrality" whereby Third World states could coexist with the USA and the Soviet Union, but should not fall under their dominance.

Libya and the Outside World

One of Qadhafi's most remarkable achievements is that Libya, having spent most of its history languishing in the shadows, suddenly erupted on to the international scene—often for all the wrong reasons.

Having absorbed the nationalist rhetoric of Gamal Abdel Nasser of Egypt, Qadhafi had been a staunch advocate of Arab unity since his youth. On Nasser's death in 1970 he saw the torch of leadership of the Pan-Arab cause passing into his hands—an idea that more mature Arab leaders regarded with derision.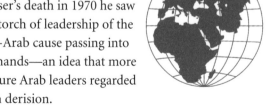

Notwithstanding he was determined to turn the dream into reality and made strenuous attempts to unite Libya with other Arab countries—firstly with Egypt and the Sudan, then with Egypt and Syria, with Egypt, with Algeria, with Tunisia, with Chad, and finally with Morocco. All of these attempts foundered, much to his chagrin.

After becoming thoroughly disillusioned with the Arab League, he sought other ways in which to project himself as a regional leader. Once the Chad conflict was resolved in 1994 by the International Court of Justice, which ruled in Chad's favor, he became a leading proponent in the Organization for African Unity, later to become, at his instigation, the African Union. But so far most African leaders have shown little enthusiasm for his proposals to set up a Pan-African government: a United States of Africa.

It is Qadhafi's relationships with the West that have earned him the greatest notoriety, particularly when his invective against Western countries was followed up with action. Libya's support for revolutionary movements, including the IRA and radical Palestinian movements, became a thorn in the flesh for countries such as Britain and the USA.

Relations with the USA started to deteriorate with the burning down of the US Embassy in Tripoli in 1978, which led to US withdrawal from Libya in 1980. In 1981 the US Sixth Fleet shot down two Libyan jet fighters over the Gulf of Sirt, which Libya claimed as its territorial waters. The USA retaliated by imposing a trade embargo, American citizens were prohibited from visiting Libya, and a number of American oil companies withdrew.

Qadhafi's call for opponents of his regime living abroad to be liquidated occasioned further alarm. After terrorist attacks at Rome and Vienna airports perpetrated by the Palestinian Abu Nidal Organization (which had links with Libya) and a bomb explosion in a West Berlin discotheque attributed to Libyan agents, President Reagan, who regarded Qadhafi as "the mad dog of the Middle East," ordered the bombing of Tripoli and Benghazi in 1986. While Qadhafi escaped unscathed, one of his daughters was killed in an air raid.

Britain broke off relations with Libya after Libyan security personnel shot a policewoman outside the Libyan People's Bureau in London in 1984. An explosion aboard an American airliner over Lockerbie in Scotland in 1988 and another on a French airliner over Niger in 1989—both allegedly set off by Libyan agents—caused universal disapproval. Libya's refusal to extradite the Lockerbie bombers for trial led to a UN

boycott of commercial flights into Libya and
economic sanctions in 1992.

Retreat from Revolution

With its oil wealth and a relatively small
population, Libya should have been in excellent
economic shape. Yet in the 1980s living
standards were declining and toward the
end of that decade the economic situation
was looking very grim. The state-owned
supermarkets that had replaced private shops
proved a disaster, failing utterly to cater to
people's needs. The army suffered a humiliating
defeat in Chad in 1987 with the loss of one-
quarter of the invasion force. Oil production
was falling with a corresponding reduction in
revenue, and Libya was finding it harder to pay
the bills for its big infrastructure projects.
International trade sanctions and an air embargo
after Lockerbie compounded the problem.

In a bid to stimulate the economy, plans were
drawn up to allow private enterprise and
commercial banking, but many of the laws to
liberalize the economy were never implemented.
Qadhafi saw that economic liberalization would
conflict with his goal of egalitarianism, while his
core supporters were opposed to anything that
would lead to a loss of privilege.

Those in charge of the oil industry made strenuous efforts to entice companies back to help revive the business. The technocrats in charge had kept their domain largely immune from the chaos that raged elsewhere, but now that the international oil market had become more competitive they found few takers.

In the late 1990s Libya began to adopt a more conciliatory stance toward its erstwhile enemies. In 1999 it agreed to surrender the Lockerbie suspects, and later compensated families of the victims of both this disaster and that of the French airliner over Niger. In 2003 it also renounced the production and use of weapons of mass destruction, including nuclear weapons, chemical agents, and mustard gas.

Little by little sanctions were lifted, diplomatic relations were resumed with Washington and London, and investment started to flow into Libya again. After years of isolation Libya was coming in from the cold.

Muammar Qadhafi remains Libya's strongman and his claim to have withdrawn from political life does not carry much credence.

Exercising, as he does, full control over the army and security services, his position seems unassailable and, like Louis XIV, he could justly boast, "*L'état, c'est moi.*" The expectation is that one of his sons will eventually succeed him. Currently the most likely contender is Saif al-Islam Qadhafi, who has run his father's charitable foundation and is regarded as a reformer.

If Libya's past history is any guide, however, one should be prepared for the unexpected. Qadhafi has poor relations with the *ulama* (the Muslim clergy) and there are a number of opposition groups, ranging from secular democrats to radical Islamists both inside and outside Libya, who are biding their time ready to exploit any weakness, just as he and other members of the Free Officers' Movement did in the 1960s.

GOVERNMENT AND POLITICS

Libya is neither a monarchy nor a republic, but a self-styled *Jamahiriya* (State of the Masses).

The General People's Congress in Tripoli formulates policy and passes laws in accordance with decisions made by twenty-six regional people's congresses. The principle is that every citizen, regardless of age or gender, should participate in the government of the country through direct consultation and consensus building. More often than not, however, it acts as a rubber stamp for Qadhafi's policies. The GPC elects the Secretary of the General People's Committees (Prime Minister), who in 2007 was Dr. Baghdadi Ali Al-Mahmudi.

General People's Committees cover the main aspects of national life (like agriculture, trade), corresponding to ministries, and their secretaries function as ministers acting as links between the committees and the Executive.

There is no General People's Committee covering defense, however; Qadhafi as Supreme Commander of the Armed Forces has complete control over defense and security matters.

There has been considerable decentralization in recent years, with the creation of 1,500 local communes (*mahallat*), each with its own budget and executive powers.

Political parties are banned in Libya, but opposition to the regime exists, with Benghazi regarded as particularly hostile to the regime. Various opposition groups are based outside Libya, of which the National Front for the Salvation of

Libya is the best resourced. There have been at least six coup attempts to remove Qadhafi that we know of, but all were put down successfully.

Qadhafi operates a highly efficient security force that keeps its ears to the ground and troublemakers at bay. He himself has no hesitation about removing ministers and other senior officials from their posts if he feels they are becoming too powerful and could pose a threat to his authority.

The legal system is undergoing revision at the present time. The Civil Code introduced in 1953 was based on the Egyptian Civil Code, which, in turn, was based on French law and incorporated aspects of *sharia* law. After the proclamation of the *Jamahiriya* the legal apparatus underwent radical changes, causing considerable confusion and uncertainty.

THE ECONOMY

After the Second World War Libya's main exports were scrap metal left over from the war, castor oil, and esparto grass (for making banknotes). Now it is petroleum, which accounts for 95 percent of the country's export earnings. Libya's main trading partners are Italy, Germany, Turkey, France, Tunisia, the UK, South Korea, and China.

The non-oil manufacturing and construction sectors account for more than 20 percent of Libya's GDP and include the production of petrochemicals, iron, steel, aluminum, cement, textiles, and handicrafts.

The agricultural sector is hampered by a lack of groundwater and only just over 1 percent of the land is cultivated. It employs around 17 percent of the workforce and the main crops are wheat, barley, olives, dates, citrus fruit, tomatoes, water melons, and vegetables. Sheep, goats, cattle, camels, and chickens are also reared. Despite massive investment in a number of large-scale agricultural schemes, it looks as if 75 percent of the country's food will continue to be imported.

Libya has considerable tourist potential, not least because of its long Mediterranean coast and its wealth of architectural sites. But perhaps as a result of Qadhafi's distrust of foreigners, the government has been slow to exploit this promising foreign currency earner.

The government controls and spends the larger part of the national income. But the inefficient allocation of resources—such as the financing of grandiose projects whose viability is unproven—means that the money is often squandered. Also, a lack of transparency renders it difficult to keep track of expenditure.

Although Qadhafi instigates periodic anticorruption drives in which he dismisses officials who appear to be feathering their nests, there is a suspicion that some of the oil wealth is siphoned off into the pockets of Qadhafi's leading supporters.

The Great Man-Made River

Many years ago a visitor remarked to his Libyan host on the benefits that the discovery of oil were bringing to his country. "How much better it would have been if we had discovered water," was the reply.

Lack of water has always been a problem for this desert nation, where rainfall is confined mainly to the coastal regions. However, the growing population along the coast has put a great strain on the local water supply. Benghazi's water table, for instance, dropped to such an extent that the city's drinking water was becoming contaminated with seawater.

Various ways of alleviating the problem were considered, including desalination plants, but the decision was made to pipe water from aquifers in the south of Libya to the coast. Work on the project, named the Great Man-Made River (GMR), began in 1984.

In 1991 the first water to be supplied by the GMR reached Benghazi, and in 1996 Tripoli too began to get water from deep desert wells. Currently around 1.7 billion gallons (6.5 million cu. m) of water flow through the pipelines daily: the original plan, since abandoned, was that the water should be used for irrigation as well as drinking.

The GMR consists of a network of pipelines, some over 600 miles (1,000 km) long and 13 feet (4 m) in diameter. By the time the project is completed it will have cost over $27 billion. It is the largest civil engineering project on earth and has been described by Qadhafi as "the eighth wonder of the world." The project is not without its critics, who fear the effect it will have on the water table in the south of Libya.

Key Dates in Libyan History

631 BCE Foundation of Cyrene

600 BCE Phoenician trading settlements of Sabratha, Oea, and Leptis Magna become colonies of Carthage

525 BCE Cyrene comes under Persian rule

331 BCE Alexander the Great retakes Cyrene for the Greeks

107 BCE Tripolitania comes under Roman control

115 CE Jewish revolt in Cyrene

435 Vandal invasion destroys Sabratha and Leptis

534 Invasion by the Byzantine general Belisarius drives out Vandals

643 Arab conquest of Libya

1510 Spain captures Tripoli

1524 Tripoli is placed under the protection of the Knights of St. John

1551 Libya comes under Ottoman control

1711 Founding of the Karamanli dynasty

1832 Ottomans regain control of Libyan provinces from the Karamanlis

1843 Grand Sanusi establishes his HQ in Cyrenaica

1911 Italy announces annexation of Tripolitania and Cyrenaica

1913 Italy attempts to occupy all three Libyan provinces

1918 Italian-Ottoman Peace Treaty gives Italy nominal control over Tripolitania and Cyrenaica

1919 Italy drafts plans for Tripolitania and Cyrenaica to have their own councils and parliaments

1922 Mussolini comes to power in Italy

1923 After Idris goes into exile in Cairo, Omar Mukhtar organizes resistance to Italians in Cyrenaica

1931 Capture and execution of Omar Mukhtar. Resistance collapses

1938 First Italian settlers arrive

1940–3 Desert War between Allies and Axis powers. Widespread destruction

1943 British military administration established in Tripolitania and Cyrenaica, and a Free French military administration in the Fezzan

1951 Libya becomes an independent kingdom under King Idris

1961 Libya exports oil for the first time

1963 Libya becomes a unitary state

1969 Coup d'état led by Muammar Qadhafi

1970 Closure of British and American bases. Appropriation of Italian properties. Nationalization of the oil companies' distribution networks

1971 Nationalization of insurance companies. Creation of Arab Socialist Union (ASU)

1973 Third Universal Theory issued. Creation of popular committees who take over media and ministries. Nationalization of oil companies

1975 Students demonstrate against Qadhafi in Benghazi. Abortive coup

1976 Abolition of ASU. Creation of General People's Congress. Publication of *The Green Book*

1977 Proclamation of the *Jamahiriya*

1978 Plans mooted for the abolition of private property, retail and private trading. Qadhafi warns *ulama* against interfering in his socialist policies and shuts down some mosques

1979 Libyan embassies become People's Bureaus. US Embassy set on fire

1980 Qadhafi orders the liquidation of Libyan dissidents. Private savings accounts banned

1981 US shoots down Libyan aircraft in the Gulf of Sirt

1984 British policewoman shot outside Libyan People's Bureau in London. UK breaks off diplomatic relations

1985 Libya expels large numbers of foreign laborers

1986 Libyan bomb explodes in West Berlin nightclub. USA bombs Tripoli and Benghazi. Leaders of G7 single out Libya as a major perpetrator of terrorism

1987 Libya announces economic liberalization. A consignment of arms sent by Libya for the IRA is found aboard the *Eksund*

1988 Pan Am airliner explodes over Lockerbie in Scotland

1989 UTA airliner explodes over Niger

1992 Two Libyans charged with Lockerbie bombing

1992 UN asks Libya to extradite Lockerbie and UTA suspects and imposes boycott of flights into Libya

1998/9 Libya agrees to surrender the Lockerbie suspects for trial in the Netherlands

1999 Libya accepts responsibility for London shooting. Diplomatic relations resumed with UK. Libya hosts OAU meeting in Sirt. Palestinian doctor and five Bulgarian nurses accused of infecting children with HIV/AIDS are imprisoned, causing international concern

2003 UN lifts sanctions. Libya renounces weapons of mass destruction and announces a liberalization program

2004 EU lifts arms embargo

2005 Libyans in exile call for removal of Qadhafi at a meeting in London

2006 USA resumes full diplomatic relations with Libya. Riot in Benghazi is infiltrated by Islamists, who burn down the Italian consulate

2007 Libya signs a defense agreement with Britain. African leaders reject Qadhafi's plans for a Pan-African government. Palestinian doctor and Bulgarian nurses are released after eight years' imprisonment. Saif al-Islam Qadhafi proposes a new constitution

chapter two

VALUES & ATTITUDES

In order to gain a proper understanding of the Libyan people, it is helpful to know something of the influences that have shaped their view of the world. Some of these are cultural—deeply ingrained traditions that have persisted over the centuries; others are a product of the more recent past, notably the upheavals Libya has experienced over the past century.

Of course, not all Libyans are the same. The desert nomad is a very different person from the sophisticated urban dweller, just as an elderly *hajji* (a person who has made the pilgrimage to Mecca) will view the world differently from a youngster. While some Libyans have a thoroughly modern cosmopolitan outlook, others hold more traditional views. But it is difficult to judge what kind of person you are dealing with from their appearance. For this reason it is best to play it safe in the early stages of a relationship and assume that all the Libyans with whom you come into contact espouse a relatively conservative outlook.

ISLAM

All Libyans are Muslims, and Islam has a strong bearing on how they conduct their lives. It is based on some basic tenets known as the Five Pillars of Islam.

> *Shahada:* The affirmation of faith that there is no god but Allah and Mohammed is his Prophet.
> *Salat:* The commitment to pray five times a day facing Mecca: at sunrise, noon, mid-afternoon, sunset, and night. On Friday people gather at the local mosque for prayer.
> *Zakat:* Offering a proportion of your income (alms) to the poor.
> *Sawm:* The annual fast during the hours of daylight in the month of Ramadan. No smoking, drinking, or eating is permitted at this time.
> The *Haj:* The pilgrimage to Mecca, which every Muslim aspires to make at least once in his or her lifetime. Libyans are forbidden to make the *Haj* before they reach the age of forty.

Importance of the Qur'an

The Muslim Holy Book, the Qur'an, meaning recitation, represents the word of God as revealed to the Prophet Mohammed in Mecca and Medina. The written records of the

Prophet's life—the Hadith—provide further instructions on how to live the godly life.

The *ulama* (Islamist jurists and scholars) are charged with interpreting the Qur'an and other writings, such as the Hadith. In Libya, however, these scholars have often found themselves in conflict with the views of Qadhafi, who has sought to reinterpret the Prophet's teachings in contemporary socialist terms.

All Muslims commit verses from the Qur'an (the suras) to heart and references to God form part of their regular speech.

Sunni and Shia

These are the two branches of Islam created as a result of a leadership struggle in the early history of the religion.

As the Prophet Mohammed had no sons, on his death the spiritual and temporal leadership of the movement, the Caliphate, passed to his father-in-law, Abu Bakr. He was succeeded by Umar, and then by Uthman. Ali, Mohammed's son-in-law, became the fourth Caliph when Uthman was murdered by the governor of Syria, Mu'awiyah, who then assassinated Ali in 661 CE and founded the Ummayad Caliphate (which derives its name from the Ummaya clan).

Hussein, Ali's son and the Prophet's grandson, raised the standard against the Ummayad dynasty and later met his end at the battle of Karbala, in present-day Iraq. This marks the beginning of the schism between the two main branches of Islam. The Shiites support the claims of Ali's successors as the legitimate authority in the Islamic world. The Sunnis, on the other hand, accept that the Caliph should be a member of the Prophet Mohammed's tribe (the Quraish) but not necessarily a lineal descendant.

The split has continued until today, although there are no great theological differences between the two movements. Shiites are very much in the minority in the Islamic world, except in Iran and Iraq, and tensions arise between the two, most notably in Iraq and Lebanon.

As far as Libya is concerned, the population is overwhelmingly Sunni. However, there were clashes between the Berbers and their Shiite rulers (the Fatimids) in the tenth century CE, and some of Qadhafi's recent pronouncements suggest that he favors Shiism.

The Sanusiya Legacy

The nineteenth century saw the beginnings of an important religious movement in Cyrenaica, when Sayyid Mohammed Ali Al-Sanusi founded a Sufi order there. Sufism is a mystical, introspective brand of Islam originating in the twelfth century, in which Muslims seek to find the truth of divine knowledge and a direct personal relationship with God. Sayyid Mohammed's White Lodge (*al-Zawia al-Beida*) is commemorated in the name of the city that now occupies that site—Beida.

The order came to be known as the Sanusiya. Its aim was to revive the pure faith and practice of the Prophet Mohammed's teaching; to restore the unity and strength of Islam by uniting the religious orders or communities (the *tariqas*) into one universal order based on the simple tenets of the Qur'an; and to teach Islam to the uneducated peoples on the fringes of the Arab world.

The practices of the order are fairly austere, though not as extreme as those of the Wahhabi sect in Saudi Arabia. Alcohol and tobacco are forbidden, and the wearing of rich clothing and jewels is frowned upon.

The educational impact of the Sanusiya was huge. Sayyid Mohammed, who became known as the Grand Sanusi, eventually moved his headquarters to Jaghbub, where he established a Muslim college that in its heyday rivaled that of Al-Azhar in Cairo. The order provided schools (the *zawias*) where none had existed before and these looked to the Qur'an for inspiration and guidance.

Sayyid Al-Mahdi, his son, carried on the tradition and by the time of his death there were eighty-eight *zawias* operating in Cyrenaica, the Fezzan, and the more isolated parts of Tripolitania, as well as in Egypt, the Hejaz, and the Sudan.

In the twentieth century the *zawias* took on a more political role, forging a link with the tribes of Cyrenaica to oppose the Italians in the First World War and its aftermath. Later they campaigned for Libyan independence. Sanusiya influence lives on in Cyrenaica, particularly among the older generation, but has never taken root in Tripolitania.

ARAB NATIONALISM

In the 1950s and 1960s President Nasser of Egypt was seen by many in the Arab world as their champion. He had overthrown the Egyptian monarchy and nationalized the Suez Canal, incurring the wrath of the British and French, who invaded Egypt in order to regain control of this asset but were later forced into a humiliating withdrawal.

Many of the younger generation throughout the Arab world were attracted to the ideal of a unified Arab state that he preached. For young Libyans, this represented a more inspiring prospect than that offered by the aging King Idris and his government, and great was the rejoicing in 1959 when Egypt and Syria merged to become the United Arab Republic.

This attempt at union proved short-lived, however, and Nasser's successors, Presidents Sadat and Mubarak, abandoned Pan-Arab rhetoric in order to address Egypt's more immediate economic concerns. Qadhafi, however, continued to champion the pan-Arab cause and embarked on several attempts to merge Libya with other Arab countries, such as Egypt, Tunisia, Chad, Morocco, and Algeria—none of which met with any success.

One facet of Arab nationalism was that Arabs should make common cause against their enemies: the former colonial powers and the enemy in their midst, Israel. Arab nationalists accuse Israel of appropriating Arab lands and depriving their fellow Arabs, the Palestinians, of their birthright. Any action Israel takes against her Arab neighbors is widely reported in Libya and can lead to anti-Israeli protests, often encouraged by the government. As a result of local anti-Israeli sentiment, Libya's Jewish community, once one of the oldest in the Arab world, has long since disappeared.

Intense political indoctrination in schools ensures that the pan-Arab dream is kept alive, although there are signs that popular support for this idea is on the wane and that virulent Islamism may be gaining ground.

ATTITUDES TO GOVERNMENT

The majority of Libyans were born since the 1969 Al-Fateh Revolution and have no notion of what life might be like under any other form of regime. In schools Qadhafi's *Green Book* is prescribed reading and his Third Universal Theory doubtless features prominently on the curriculum.

How do people react to this? One senses that nowadays the revolutionary flame burns less brightly than it once did and that many Libyans are bored with politics. Their attitude to the government is not unlike that of people in Soviet bloc countries during the Cold War: they are apathetic toward politics, realizing that they are powerless to change matters. They shrug their shoulders at Qadhafi's latest pronouncements, and the majority could not care less whether he stays in power or is replaced.

Although Libya is richer than its neighbors, people do not have a great deal of disposable wealth of their own; it is the government that spends the oil revenues. Salaries remained static for over two decades and, despite recent adjustments in pay and allowances, people still grumble. But they also accept that things could be worse and retreat into the bosom of their families. Those who cannot stand the government leave to join the 100,000 or so Libyan exiles abroad.

ATTITUDES TO THE WEST

The bitter experience of Italian colonialism, when large numbers of Libyans were deported or annihilated, continues to color Libyan attitudes to European countries to a greater or lesser degree. Qadhafi has never hesitated in the past to tar all Western countries with the same colonialist brush. As a consequence relationships between the Libyan government and the West have been somewhat bumpy since the overthrow of the monarchy in 1969.

It had not always been like this, however. King Idris had pro-British leanings and allowed Britain and the USA to maintain bases on Libyan soil. (The Wheelus airbase near Tripoli was one of the largest US bases outside America.) But, as we have seen, not all Libyans at the time supported the pro-Western stance of the Idris government, and in fact many of the younger generation were attracted to the anti-Western rhetoric of Radio Cairo.

After his coup d'état Qadhafi set about ridding the country of Western "colonial" influences: closing down the British and American bases as well as foreign cultural centers and libraries, and expelling thousands of the remaining Italian residents. After the American bombing of Tripoli and Benghazi in 1986, English teaching in schools was stopped for a period of two years.

The climate is changing now, though. The once reviled Italians are Libya's most important trading partners and are welcomed everywhere; Britain has reopened its cultural center in Tripoli; and Western goods find a ready market in Libya.

Libyan educational institutions are anxious to cultivate links with those in the West and increasing numbers of Libyans are going to Europe for their education rather than to other Arab countries. Libyans are starting to reject the anti-Western rhetoric of the past and are generally welcoming to strangers.

ATTITUDES TO THE ARAB WORLD

Libyans share a common language with their neighbors in the Arab world as well as the Muslim faith, naturally creating a strong bond. This tie is reinforced by the presence of Arabs from other countries living and working in Libya, including a large number of teachers and lecturers. Intermarriage with other Arab nationals is not uncommon and Libyans regard other Arabs as their "brothers." Arabs are not subject to the same strict immigration controls as other nationals (though this could change as Libya takes action to stem the potential terrorist threat) and many have flocked into the country either to escape trouble at home or in order to enjoy the better standard of living that Libya's oil wealth offers them.

Historically, the Cyrenaicans have always identified closely with Egypt. Indeed, many of their forebears sought asylum there during the Italian occupation. The Tripolitanians have traditionally had closer ties with Tunisia and the other Maghreb countries.

Political relations with other Arab countries have been fraught at times, often because of Qadhafi's frustration at their failure to work together to advance the cause of Arab nationalism and take up arms against Israel. As we have seen, attempts to link Libya up with Egypt, Tunisia, and Syria—to name but a few—have failed to get off the ground and there have been several disagreements with the Arab League. Libya also has a long-standing territorial dispute with Algeria, having laid claim to more than 12,350 square miles (32,000 sq. km) of land in the southeast of that country.

ATTITUDES TO AFRICA AND AFRICANS

In recent years Qadhafi has enjoyed greater success in promoting the cause of Pan-Africanism than he ever did with Pan-Arabism, but his dream of an African superstate looks unlikely to get off the ground. His relations with Libya's closest neighbors have been problematical. There is an ongoing territorial dispute with Niger regarding 9,650 square miles (25,000 sq. km) of the Tommo region. In the 1970s Qadhafi made an abortive military incursion into the Aozou Strip in Chad to gain access to its minerals and gain political influence.

Libyans tend to be less than enthusiastic about Africa and Qadhafi's African policy in particular. They resent the large amounts of money from the Libyan treasury being poured into bodies such as the African Union.

They also oppose the influx of African immigrants from south of the Sahara, some of them fellow Muslims, even though they are prepared to take jobs that no Libyan would consider doing. They blame them for any crimes that are committed and for introducing diseases like HIV into Libya, whether it is true or not. One senses an undercurrent of racism in their attitudes.

ATTITUDES TO WOMEN

While in certain quarters women are regarded as inferior to men in mind, body, and spirit, in the eyes of the law they enjoy equal status with men in modern Libya. But old attitudes die hard, and the ideal Arab woman is expected to be modest, decorous, and virtuous in order not to bring dishonor on her family.

The government has been leading the way in the cause of female emancipation. Until the 1960s you would see women going about veiled—either from top to toe or with their faces covered with a black scarf. Nowadays veiled women are the exception rather than the rule, though there is a trend among women of a fundamentalist disposition to wear the *hejab* (hair covering). Unlike in some Arab countries, Libyan women have equal rights, including the right to equal pay for equal work. They have the right to vote, own property, and participate in politics.

A woman cannot be married against her will; and if her father is unwilling to give his consent to a marriage she may apply to the court for permission to marry. She also has the right to seek a divorce. In the event of a divorce it is the woman rather than the man who is deemed to have the right to custody of any children from the marriage and possession of the marital home.

The government has led the way in female emancipation despite opposition from traditionalists but, although Libya acceded to the Convention of the Elimination of All Forms of Discrimination against Women in 1989, there is the proviso that practices should not conflict with *sharia* law (which definitely does discriminate).

When a woman reaches menopause she becomes an *azuz* and is automatically accorded greater status.

Bedouin women have more freedom. They usually go about unveiled and take a full part in tribal life. This is also true of women in rural communities, though care is taken to shield them from contact with strangers. In Tuareg society, by contrast, it is the women who are dominant, while their menfolk go about "veiled" (in blue, indigo-dyed fabric, to shield them from the desert sun).

WORK ETHIC

Like most Mediterranean peoples Libyans have a relaxed attitude to work. They see no point in rushing around to meet deadlines. Work is not the most important thing in the world and matters can always wait until tomorrow—*bukra* in Arabic. There is also an element of fatalism, particularly among the more pious. Everything is dependent on God's will, and things either happen or they don't; nobody can make things happen.

Inevitably you will find exceptions to the rule, notably among Libyans who have lived and worked abroad and who would like their country to be more dynamic. But the relaxed attitude has certain benefits, especially in the heat of summer, when a person really needs to slow down and unwind.

FESTIVALS & TRADITIONS

Every country observes holidays spread throughout the year, when businesses close down for a day or longer, such as Thanksgiving in the USA and Easter in the UK—and so it is with Libya. Families welcome these as an opportunity to have a break in their routine and perhaps a day out, a family get-together, or simply relax. Religious festivals are of particular significance to Libyans and we need to differentiate them from national holidays.

In Libya, as in most Muslim countries, there are two calendars in operation: the lunar calendar of approximately 354 days and the solar calendar of 365 or 366 days. Religious festivals follow the lunar calendar, so in terms of the solar calendar they occur ten days earlier each year. (Other cultures that use the lunar calendar, such as the Chinese, add days or the occasional month to their years in order to keep them in step with the seasons and the solar calendar.) Libya's national (nonreligious) holidays are fixed according to the solar, or Gregorian, calendar, which is in general use throughout the world.

NATIONAL HOLIDAYS

These, on the whole, are regarded as less important than religious holidays, and most have become just days off work, rather than opportunities for celebration. Interestingly, Libya is one of just a few countries that no longer marks the day it gained independence—December 24. This is presumably because of the view that it did not become truly independent of Western influence until the 1969 Revolution. Most of these holidays commemorate events that have happened since the Revolution.

March 2: Declaration of the Jamahiriya

This commemorates the proclamation of the new constitution in 1977, creating a new style of government by the people.

March 22: Arab League Day
The Arab League, a political association to which most Arab states belong, was founded on this day in 1945.

March 28: British Evacuation Day
This commemorates the closure of British bases and withdrawal of British troops in 1970.

June 11: Evacuation Day
This commemorates the closure of the US airbase at Wheelus and the withdrawal of American troops in 1970.

July 23: Revolution Day
This commemorates the day in 1952 when a military coup in Egypt toppled the government of King Farouk and led to Colonel Nasser's rise to power.

September 1: National Day
Libya's national day and the most important secular holiday in the Libyan calendar commemorates Qadhafi's coup d'état in 1969. In addition to speeches and parades there are various types of entertainment, including musical and folklore events. The festivities can last up to a week.

October 7: Italian Evacuation Day
This commemorates the day in 1970 when the Italian community was "invited" to leave and their land repossessed.

October 26: Day of Mourning
This looks back to the Italian invasion of Libya in 1911 and the ruthless oppression of Libyans during the Italian occupation.

Since holidays are subject to change it would be sensible to check with local people on which of these days businesses and government offices are closed.

RELIGIOUS FESTIVALS
Religious festivals are generally more highly regarded by Libyans than the official holidays, in much the same way as Christmas is in the West. The *eids* (*eid* means feast) are particularly important and an opportunity for family gatherings.

Ras as-Sana: New Year's Day
Meaning "head of the year," this is the Islamic new year. It is celebrated as a public holiday on the first day of the first month (Moharram) of the Islamic calendar .

Ashura

The tenth day of Moharram is also celebrated;
it commemorates the assassination of Hussein
Ibn Ali, the grandson of the Prophet
Mohammed.

Eid al-Moulad

The twelfth day of the third month of the Islamic
year (Rabi Al-Awal) celebrates the birth of the
Prophet Mohammed and is a great family
celebration.

Ramadan

The ninth month of the Muslim year is a
particularly holy period and commemorates the
time that the word of God, as represented in the
Qu'ran, was revealed to the Prophet Mohammed
by the Angel Gabriel.

This is a time of fasting (*sawm*).
Between sunrise and sunset Muslims
abstain from eating, drinking,
smoking, and sexual activity.
Exemptions are made for children,
pregnant women, the elderly, and
travelers. During the day all cafés and restaurants
are closed, except those catering to non-Muslims,
who are under no obligation to observe the fast.
However, when eating or drinking you should do
so discreetly and not in full view of everybody.

When the daily fast is over there is usually a signal—in Tripoli a cannon is fired—to signify the fast is over and people settle down to their evening meal. This is known as the *iftar* (breaking of the fast). Some Libyans begin, following Mohammed's example, by eating dates and milk, but as the evening wears on more substantial fare is provided and there is usually plenty of partying. It is sometimes said that more food is consumed during the Ramadan fast than during any other month of the Islamic year.

While all-night parties are popular, most Muslims manage to snatch a little sleep before eating a predawn meal, known as the *suhur*, which has to keep them going for the whole day. It is customary for the devout to spend the twenty-seventh night of Ramadan at the mosque in prayer or listening to the Qu'ran being read.

Ramadan is an intensely spiritual experience that is taken very seriously by Muslims, far more than the period of Lent is by Christians. However, the long hours of abstinence, especially in summer when the days are long and the weather is hot, can cause people to be become moody and ill-tempered, and smokers may suffer withdrawal symptoms. It is not a month where you can hope to achieve much, since people are often distracted and find it difficult to concentrate on their work.

Eid al-Fitr

This three-day festival marks the end of the Ramadan fast and it is customary to have prayers at sunrise at the mosque, normally followed by a celebratory family meal, reminiscent of the traditional Christmas meal in the West. This is a time for exchanging gifts, buying new clothes for the children, and traveling home to see loved ones.

Eid al-Adha

The Feast of the Sacrifice, sometimes referred to as Eid al-Kabeer (Great Feast) commemorates Ibrahim's sacrifice to God of a ram instead of his son Ismail (a version of the biblical story of Abraham and Isaac). It marks the beginning of the month of pilgrimage when the devout undertake their spiritual journey to Mecca. The festivities usually involve the ritual slaughter of a lamb and donating some of the meat to the poor. This is another excuse for a family get-together and the holiday lasts three or four days.

FAMILY CELEBRATIONS

Birth and Circumcision

Although the birth of a child is greeted with excitement and joy, there are not normally any special celebrations. When a boy is circumcised, however, the event is usually accompanied by a party and the exchange of presents.

Weddings

A wedding celebrates not merely the union of two people but two families. At one time the celebrations would last for a week. Nowadays they tend to be shorter—typically three days—starting on a Wednesday.

On this day the family of the groom present the bride with gold and other gifts. Some will be very traditional, such as incense, Libyan costumes, and henna, which is applied to the bride's hands and feet in traditional designs. And then the partying starts, and it is not unusual for the music and dancing to continue until the dawn.

On the Thursday the bride celebrates her wedding with her family and friends, and then is taken to the bridegroom's home. On the Friday there is more festivity with female musicians and dancers entertaining the female guests while male musicians perform for the men. The women show their joy with a loud trilling noise and play the *darbouka* (a type of drum).

Weddings tend to be held in people's homes, and sometimes tents are erected to offer more room. Plenty of eating takes place, and the evening meals on Wednesday and Thursday often feature rice pilaf and various side dishes. A sweet drink made from almond milk is traditional.

Funerals

After death the deceased's body is washed and clothed in clean linen and buried within twenty-four hours, if possible, with the right side facing Mecca. Only the menfolk attend the ceremony, leaving the women of the family to express their grief at the home of the deceased.

LOCAL FESTIVALS

A number of local festivals occur at different times of the year and usually prove to be lively affairs. The oases of Libya seem to be particularly keen on festivals to celebrate the date harvest.

The Ghadames Festival, which takes place in October or November, offers days of music, singing, and dancing as well as displays of horsemanship.

The Ghat Festival at the end of December is a notable Tuareg event noted for its camel races, poetry recitations, as well as its music.

Tripoli also takes on something of a carnival atmosphere during the Tripoli International Fair. In addition to being an important trade fair, it offers various forms of jollification, including an amusement park and live music.

chapter four

MAKING FRIENDS

Although the importance of the family has been emphasized, we need to recognize that Libyans also have a circle of friends who play an important part in their lives. Many friendships are formed at an early age—at school or college—and last a lifetime.

Friendship is based on trust and this can take time to take root. If you find that the Libyans you meet are reserved and undemonstrative, you should not assume hostility on their part. Partly as a consequence of the upheavals since the Revolution of 1969, they tend to be somewhat wary of strangers. Moreover, the regime has fostered a distrust of foreigners that will take time to eradicate.

So do not expect the same openness and frankness you find in Egypt or Tunisia, for instance. Libya is not a place for "instant relationships," but if you can establish trust, everything is possible. You may well find, particularly among the younger generation, a more positive attitude to strangers.

SOCIALIZING WITH LIBYANS

If you are working in Libya, you will be socializing with Libyans on a daily basis, and probably discussing work problems or exchanging advice. Unlike in the West, people tend to disperse to their homes at the end of the working day rather than linger on. There may be the occasional work or office get-together, however, though these may seem very sedate by European standards.

The people whom you will find most approachable are those with whom you share a common interest, professional or recreational. There will be Libyans who have spent time in your own country, who will be keen to meet you and keep up with the latest news. They will be in a position to view Libya from your perspective and may be able to offer a helping hand. Such help should be gratefully accepted. It is, after all, essential to understand Libyan society and be sensitive to the various rules and conventions. These will vary according to the region where you are living and the background of the people you are dealing with.

You need, for example, to accept that the sexes live separate lives and, while it is possible for a male foreigner to have male Libyan friends, families may look askance if you attempt to strike up a friendship with a daughter of the family. Female foreigners should aspire to have female Libyan friends, even if young Libyan men take an interest in them. Married people may find that they can fit into Libyan society more easily.

It is, however, impossible to lay down hard and fast views, given that Libya has changed a lot in the past fifty years and is likely to undergo even more rapid changes in the years ahead. Be prepared to seek advice on relationships from those who live in the country and have a proper understanding of cultural differences.

LEARNING ARABIC

If you really want to make an impact on Libyans, you should arrive with a good command of Arabic. Even if you are planning to spend only a short time in Libya, it would be of benefit to learn some Arabic

before you go. For Europeans it is a hard language to learn, since its script, vocabulary, and grammar are unfamiliar.

If you are paying a short visit it will probably be easiest if you opt for a course in colloquial Arabic, in which the words are transcribed into Roman script. Take care that you choose a style of Arabic that will be readily understood in Libya. Gulf Arabic or Moroccan Arabic would sound strange to a Libyan ear; Egyptian or Levantine Arabic are far more acceptable.

Many language schools and colleges in Europe and North America offer introductory courses in Arabic, some of them intensive, including the School of Oriental and African Studies (SOAS) in London. If you would like to study in the Arab world, there are numerous courses available, including those run by the American Universities in Cairo and Beirut and the Institut Bourguiba des Langues Vivantes in Tunis. Private tuition is available in Tripoli and Benghazi, and educational institutions are prepared to arrange courses where there is sufficient demand. (See pages 152–4 and 160–3 for a very brief introduction to the Arabic language and some useful words and phrases.)

MAKING CONVERSATION

Small talk and gossip are a favourite pastime of most Libyans, so if you want to get on with them well it makes sense to cultivate the art of conversation. Naturally, the last thing you want to do is commit faux pas or say anything that will create a bad impression.

Make allowance, when conversing in English, for the fact that the people you are talking to  are not native speakers of your language (no matter how good their English may sound) and they may not always grasp what you are talking about if you use a lot of idioms or colloquialisms, or indulge in irony. Attempt to speak plainly and clearly in order to avoid misunderstandings.

Don't try to dominate the conversation, but allow them to hold forth. Listen respectfully to their comments and avoid arguments. A good listener is often a better conversationalist than a prolific talker.

You'll need to be particularly circumspect about topics of conversation. Some are likely to give offense, particularly to less sophisticated Libyans, while others are perfectly safe.

Taboo Topics

Politics is not an option, particularly the politics of Libya, unless you know the person you are talking to very well indeed. Although criticism of Qadhafi is common, especially among the young, it would be unwise for a foreigner to join in, and could even land you in prison on a charge of subversion. You might also find yourself in difficult straits if the conversation turns to international politics and you find yourself having to defend the policies of your own government.

Another sensitive subject is Islam. You should steer away from debates about the respective merits of Islam and other religions for fear of being thought to be belittling their deeply held faith. There is plenty of room for misunderstandings in matters theological. You may feel awkward, especially if Libyans try to convert you or express opinions about your own religion that you know to be incorrect. Qadhafi himself is not averse to making public pronouncements on theological matters—but as a stranger you would be unwise to follow his example. There is no harm, however, in correcting any misconceptions Libyans may have about your own religion, provided you do not start to proselytize.

Jokes are best avoided. It is not that Libyans lack a sense of humor, but humor, unless it is very straightforward, does not travel well.

Recommended Topics

Libyans enjoy talking about their family and especially the achievements of their children. (Male visitors, however, should be careful not to show too great an interest in the womenfolk of the household. In very traditional households it is best not to mention them at all unless they are referred to in the conversation.)

There are plenty of other topics, though, that can be discussed freely. Sports, especially soccer,

are popular among men, and you may find that they are far more knowledgeable about European or US teams than you are. Television, films, music, and food are good, neutral topics for discussion, and there is always that perennial standby, the weather.

Libyans will often be eager to hear your opinions, particularly regarding Libya and your experiences in their country, and you should be as complimentary as possible. Like all of us, they appreciate flattery.

Many are curious about the outside world and may ply you with questions about the international political scene and life where you come from. Now that young Libyans are starting to go abroad for their studies once more, you may be asked about educational establishments in your country.

chapter five

DAILY LIFE

Libya may be part of the African continent
and the Arab world, but the differences tend to
outweigh the similarities. Like most of the others
it is a young country with a youthful population,
but there the similarity ends. Libyans are on
average five times better off than their neighbors,
and life expectancy is close to European standards:
74.5 years for men, 79 years for women.

They also benefit from living in a welfare state
that provides free health care and free education
for all. Food is subsidized and, surprisingly
perhaps, so are cars. This has given rise to a
dependency culture—the expectation that the
state will provide everything—and there is a
general unwillingness to rock the boat.

Libyans have come a very long way in two
generations from a predominantly rural, tribal
society to one based mainly in the towns. In the
1950s only 25 percent of the population lived in
urban areas, whereas now it is 80 percent. Over a
century there have been even more striking
changes. In the early twentieth century 10 percent

of the population were nomads and 30 percent led a seminomadic existence, much as Qadhafi's parents and grandparents did. Nowadays the overwhelming majority of Libyans are settled.

THE FAMILY

Family life plays a central role in Libyan society. Libyans prefer to live in family units rather than alone, and the importance of the family unit has been fully supported by the government. Because of the political upheaval experienced since the Revolution family loyalties have been strengthened, and tribal loyalties, which might have been expected to diminish as society became more urbanized, still linger on.

A traditional Libyan household will consist of a man, his wife, their unmarried children, and other dependents. The man is the decision maker and assumes responsibility for the family, much as a Victorian paterfamilias would have done. The concept of honor is important and everybody is expected to pull together to protect the reputation of the family.

Traditionally the wife and other womenfolk were entrusted with the domestic duties: cooking, cleaning, shopping, and looking after the children. Even today a male Libyan who helps with the housework is very much the exception. But the modern Libyan woman is not necessarily willing to take on a subservient role. Many make good use of the educational opportunities open to them and increasing numbers have jobs and professions outside the home.

LIBYANS AT HOME

The home is important to all Libyans, who regard it as is a refuge from the hostile world outside. The traditional Libyan home would have been built around a central courtyard with rooms leading off it. It would have been unusual to have windows on the ground floor looking outside. Each house would have a reception room set apart as the public space in the home, where the head of the household would entertain his friends and visitors. The Karamanli Museum in Tripoli offers an idea of how domestic living used to be arranged.

Urban living has changed things. Libyans

are more likely to live in multistory apartments these days. Those who can afford houses usually live in two-story villas with flat roofs that can be used for a number of different functions: as a children's play area, a place for parties, or for more mundane activities such as hanging out the wash.

GROWING UP IN LIBYA

Libyans are fond of children and they tend to pamper them, showering them with gifts and boasting to others about their achievements. And they are bound to have lots of adoring relations just dying to see them. Libyan fathers are particularly anxious to have a male heir. Families prefer to look after their children themselves rather than rely on the services of a nanny, but nursery schools are now starting to spring up.

Primary and Secondary Education

Education has a top priority and is free and compulsory for children between the ages of six and fifteen. There has been a considerable investment in education over the years and the results are impressive. Libya's literacy rate of more than 80 percent for adults over fifteen is probably the highest in Africa.

Primary school lasts from six to twelve years, after which pupils go to the lower secondary school. If they pass the graduating exam they can proceed to the upper secondary level. The curriculum is controlled by the National Center for Educational Planning, which makes sure that students are thoroughly grounded in the philosophy of the Revolution. At one time many girls missed out on education, but nowadays all of them attend school and continue there longer than their male counterparts. The average Libyan girl has ten years of education as opposed to eight for a boy.

There has been an increase in private school provision in Tripoli, including a new school run by the international school group GEMS Education. There are a number of community schools serving the children of Pakistani, Turkish, Egyptian, French, British, German, and Italian expatriates. Among them are the British Community School; the so-called International School of Martyrs, set up by foreign oil companies in the 1960s to provide education for the children of their expatriate staff, which follows the Irish School curriculum; and Tripoli College, once described as "Eton of Libya," which follows the British school curriculum. These schools take a certain proportion of Libyan pupils in addition to expatriate children.

Further and Higher Education

From the upper secondary level many Libyans go on to one of the many vocational institutes or to higher education. The country has twelve state universities, of which the oldest and largest are Garyounis University with 60,000 students in Benghazi and Al-Fateh University in Tripoli with 115,000 students. There is also a University of Tripoli and a University of Benghazi, both private institutions.

The country is still not self-sufficient in teaching staff and relies on teachers from other countries of the Arab world, notably Egypt, to make up the numbers. A few science and medical courses are taught through the medium of English, but for most subjects the language of instruction is Arabic.

Tripoli has an estimated 150 language schools providing classes in English and other languages, including one run by the British Council. Provision in Benghazi is more limited. Oil companies provide training in English and technical trades for their Libyan staff in order to reduce Libya's dependence on foreign workers.

Conscription and the Armed Forces

When young people—both male and female—reach the age of seventeen they become liable for conscription into the armed forces, which is done on a selective basis. At any one time there are 25,000 conscripts in the 45,000-strong army. There are also 40,000 members in the people's militia, which is a reserve force.

Conscription is not at all popular with young people, and there has been quite considerable resistance to the idea of women soldiers, although Qadhafi is very keen on them. Libya's leader is often accompanied by a fifty-strong female bodyguard.

THE WORLD OF WORK

With increasing numbers of young Libyans entering the labor market, finding a job is starting to become a problem, and Libya's unemployment rate is hovering around the 30 percent mark.

The problem is compounded by the fact that young Libyans want prestigious jobs in offices rather than what they regard as menial jobs on building sites and elsewhere, which provide employment for immigrant workers. Government jobs are far from being well-paid, however, and by 2006 salary rates had remained frozen for twenty-five years. Many Libyans supplement their income with part-time work and small business ventures.

In the past the government embarked on ambitious large-scale industrial and agricultural projects only to find it necessary to recruit skilled workers from abroad. Libyan agriculture has had to import workers from Egypt and Africa because of the migration of rural people to the towns. When foreign workers were expelled in the 1980s in order to restore the country's balance of trade some facilities had difficulties in functioning.

The presence of large numbers of foreign workers in the country who are willing to work for lower wages than any Libyan prompted a backlash in the late 1990s. Jobless Libyans provoked riots against African immigrants whom they perceived as the main culprits, and some African workers were killed.

Despite heavy investment in vocational and other types of education, there is still a shortage of skills. Frequent and ill-considered changes to the educational curriculum are held partly to blame for this. The government expects foreign companies to train their Libyan staff with a view to eventually phasing out foreign workers.

THE POSITION OF WOMEN

Libyan society, like most Arab cultures, tends to be male dominated, yet the Revolutionary government has been very supportive of women's rights. As we have seen, a girl cannot be married against her will, and if her father is unwilling to give his consent to a marriage she may apply to the court for permission to marry. She also has the right to seek a divorce. While polygamy is permitted, a husband has to seek permission from the first wife before he can marry another.

Women have equal status with men under the law, including the right to equal pay for equal work. They have the right to vote and own property and participate in politics.

Nowadays women are encouraged to take jobs and play a part in the social life of the country, though many exhibit a certain reticence or lack sufficient self-confidence to do so. There are women working in education and health care, in the police and army, in the government and judiciary. Even so, they still only make up 20 percent of the workforce.

The proportions may well change given that both sexes have equal access to education nowadays. In higher education, it seems, women students outnumber the men. "Female students have a high receptivity and readiness to venture into male dominated occupations," according to a recent report. So perhaps girl power will win out in the end.

LOVE AND MARRIAGE

In the past premarital romantic relationships were frowned upon but, in an increasingly urbanized society where young women and men come into daily contact with each other—in the workplace, at school, and at university—dating is becoming more acceptable. A certain amount of subterfuge is exercised, however, and meetings tend to take place in secret without the knowledge of parents or siblings. Cell phones are proving to be an asset to those who wish to arrange meetings away from prying eyes.

In Libya it is taken for granted that people will get married, and there is a deeply rooted tradition to keep such unions, if at all possible, within the extended family unit. One tradition is that the eldest son of a family has the automatic right to marry his paternal uncle's eldest daughter. Only if he waives this right is she free to marry someone else. This rule may be falling into abeyance, though, since according to Libyan law no girl can be forced into marrying a particular person and she has legal redress if pressure is brought to bear. Also, younger people want the freedom to choose their own partners.

Nevertheless, the preference, certainly among the older generation, is for sons and daughters to marry someone from within the wider family circle, since marriage is looked upon as the union of two families. The bride, who is expected to be a virgin, will be at least twenty years old, and sexual relationships before marriage are strictly taboo. The bridegroom is likely to be some years older, since he (often with the help of his family) needs to amass sufficient capital to pay his would-be in-laws a bride-price. The more highly esteemed the bride, the greater the amount of money involved. It is assumed that a married couple will wish to start a family as quickly as possible.

If a Muslim woman wishes to marry a man who is not a Muslim, he is expected by law to convert to her faith. Conversion is not obligatory if the woman is non-Muslim, but the children are expected to be brought up as Muslims.

SHOPPING

The socialist experiment involving the abolition of private retailing and its replacement by government-owned supermarkets proved to be a disaster. Now that the retail trade is back in the private sector shortages are few and most goods are plentiful.

Despite the advent of supermarkets most Libyans enjoy the more traditional modes of shopping, particularly the *souk* and markets. Some districts are named after the markets that take place there, for example, Souk el-Jouma (Friday market).

The practice of haggling is less common than elsewhere in the Middle East. The vendor usually sets a price and it is up to the customer to beat him down. Stallholders tend to charge foreigners more than they would locals. However, in the more modern retail sector fixed prices are the norm.

LAW AND ORDER

Since Qadhafi came to power there have been half a dozen attempts to overthrow him. That none has succeeded so far is a tribute to the tight security in operation in the country. There are checkpoints on some of the roads and security checks are often conducted at public installations and even hotels. People are expected to carry proper documentation around with them at all times.

chapter six

TIME OUT

Libyans are sociable people. They seem never to turn down an opportunity to get together, and enjoy making new friends. The workplace is just as good for socializing as a café, restaurant, or park; there is no great divide between the worlds of work and leisure, as can happen in the West.

On their days off families like to pay visits to relations or friends or go to one of a number of vacation villages and resorts along the coast. In the evenings men will often stroll around town meeting up with friends at public meeting places. Women, by contrast, tend to stay in their homes and entertain there.

Libyans enjoy travel and the embargo on international flights hit them hard. The restoration of air links with the outside world now means they can travel around more easily. Tunisia and Malta are favorite destinations for Tripolitanians, and cosmopolitan centers, such as London, Rome, and Paris, where many of them have relatives, are extremely popular.

Libyan women are particularly fond of visiting Western countries as they feel able to move about more freely.

FOOD AND DRINK

Libyan food is best described as plain and tasty rather than elaborate and gourmet. Libyans do not have the tradition of eating out, though things are beginning to change with the advent of fast-food chains. Instead they tend to eat at home and this is certainly the best place to sample authentic Libyan cuisine.

The first-time visitor is unlikely to receive an invitation to eat at home with a family. If you are, you can consider yourself highly honored. The traditional way of eating is to sit cross-legged on a cushion at a low table on which is placed a large tray or platter containing the food. It is up to those present to help themselves. The food in the center of the platter is regarded as an offering of thanks to heaven and is never eaten. Bread is usually eaten with the meal and it is quite in order to break pieces off the loaf and dip them in the soup.

The evening meal is usually the main meal of the day and it is customary in devout households to say a prayer (the equivalent of grace) before the meal. A bowl of perfumed water may be passed around for ritual cleansing; it is the custom to dip in just three fingers.

While some hotels and restaurants serve typical Libyan cuisine, the majority tend to offer standard international dishes. Most of the chefs are from other Arab countries, notably Morocco.

Traditional Cuisine

Libyan cuisine has been subject to a number of influences over the centuries: Mediterranean, Turkish, and Arab. In Tripolitania, Italian pasta dishes and food with a Mediterranean flavor are popular, while Cyrenaicans look eastward to Egypt for culinary inspiration.

Lamb and chicken are favorites, and beef is also eaten widely. Pork, however, is *haram* (forbidden for religious reasons) and, strangely, despite the abundant marine life in the coastal waters, fish dishes are the exception rather than the rule.

A Libyan Feast

One of the most typical Libyan dishes is *sharba.* *Sharba Libya* is a thick broth containing lamb, spices, onions, vegetables, mint, and tomato paste.

There are variations, including *sharba dajaaj* (chicken broth) and *sharba hout* (seafood broth).

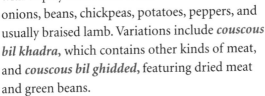

Another dish that can be found all over North Africa is *couscous*, which is steamed semolina (or buckwheat) served with a spicy stew made from onions, beans, chickpeas, potatoes, peppers, and usually braised lamb. Variations include *couscous bil khadra*, which contains other kinds of meat, and *couscous bil ghidded*, featuring dried meat and green beans.

Also widely eaten are:

- *Shatshouka*, which consists of chopped lamb and vegetables in tomato sauce and egg
- *Borek*, a Turkish dish consisting of rolls of light pastry usually stuffed with minced meat and spinach
- *Falafel*, which are mashed chickpeas and spices rolled into balls and then fried. These are often served in sandwich form on pita bread
- *Kufte*, which are like burgers made from ground meat flavored with spices and freshly chopped herbs. Usually served with potatoes and salad.

Stuffed vine leaves, *bouillabaisse* (seafood stew), and marinated and grilled vegetables are also prominently featured on the Libyan table.

Drink

Before the Revolution Libya produced its own wine, beer, and spirits, but this is no longer the case. Prohibition is now in force, which means that Libyans and visitors alike have to make do with sweet fizzy drinks, fruit juice, mineral water, or nonalcoholic beer. Beware of spirits made in illicit stills, which can be lethal.

It is possible that one day wine and beer will flow again at a new tourist development that is planned on the coast near the Tunisian border, though religious opposition could well thwart such plans.

Arabic coffee—Turkish coffee, by another name—is served in small cups. Half the cup is taken up with coffee grounds and you should firstly stir the coffee and then leave time for these to settle. Instant coffee is also available if you specify Nescafé.

Libyan Tea Parties

Tea drinking is a very popular pastime, and may involve elaborate ceremonial, with guests being served three small glasses of tea prepared in front of them as they sit cross-legged at a low table.

There is often a choice between green tea and black tea. Libyans refer to black tea as *shahi ahmar* (red tea) because, if you hold the glass of tea up to the light, it will appear red.

The first glass is plain strong tea, which has been put into a teapot and boiled. It is then strained into a second teapot and large quantities of sugar added. It is then poured back and forth between the teapot and a metal cup until it begins to froth and is then poured into the tea glasses and handed round with cookies and cakes. As a person finishes his glass everyone says *Sahah* (Your health), to which the response is *Salmak* (And yours).

The glasses are passed back to be rinsed ready for the second round. This tea is prepared in a similar way with mint added.

The third glass of tea is not frothy. Instead the glasses are filled with peanuts and almonds and the tea poured over them. Sometimes incense is burned at the end.

ENTERTAINMENT

Anyone coming to Libya hoping to enjoy a vibrant nightlife will be disappointed. There is a conspicuous lack of commercial entertainment venues, but live music is played in

some restaurants and hotels, notably the
Corinthia in Tripoli.

No party, wedding, or festival would be
complete without communal singing and
dancing, but at other times people rely on home
entertainment: TV, radio, CDs, DVDs, and
computer games.

The Libyan media are state controlled for
the most part and somewhat tedious. For this
reason people switch to satellite channels such
as CNN and the Qatar-based Al-Jazeera for
news of the world outside, and to Italian and
Egyptian TV stations for sports and other
entertainment.

In the evening women generally stay at
home while the menfolk go out to meet up
with their friends. You see them
strolling around the parks
and streets and gathering in
coffeehouses, where they play
games of cards, backgammon, chess,
or dominoes. Some smoke water
pipes—known as *sheesha* or
nargila. Incidentally, there are no
restrictions on smoking cigarettes
in public places as occurs in
some health-conscious
Western countries.

MUSIC AND DANCE

In Libya, as in all Arab countries, Umm
Kolthum—the Egyptian Edith Piaf—remains
popular despite the fact that she died in 1975.
Another female singer who continues to
have an impact is Fairouz from the
Lebanon, now living in retirement. But
Libya has plenty of homegrown talent
these days, such as Ayman Al-Aathar,
the reggae band Tyre Alarbiat, and the
band Zoukra, who perform music
reminiscent of Moroccan trance music.
Bwahbab, an elderly blind singer who sings
traditional Libyan songs, finds favor with the
older generation. Other popular singers are Firkat
Al-Hurru, Saif Al-Nasser, Ahmed Fakroun, and
Masoud. Nasser Al-Mizdawi, whose music is a
fusion of Arab music and Western pop, has an
enthusiastic following among the younger people.

As elsewhere in the Arab world, orchestras tend
to be a blend of Western instruments (notably
violins and wind instruments), the traditional *oud*
(a string instrument akin to a lute), and a *tabla*
(hand drums). Other traditional instruments you
may come across include the *darbuk* (a type of
drum), the *zokra* (similar to bagpipes), bamboo
flutes, and tambourines. Sometimes the music is
accompanied by complex clapping rhythms.

If traditional Arab music sounds strange to a Western ear, bear in mind that it uses quarter tones, whereas notes in Western music progress in semitones. Live performances are not very common, but musicians play at parties and weddings and are available on CDs and DVDs.

LITERATURE

Libya has a strong tradition of oral poetry, as is common in countries with a nomadic tradition. There are regular radio broadcasts devoted to poetry readings, and poetry recitals are sometimes held in galleries and at festivals, such as the Ghat Festival. Written literature is a more recent phenomenon, with its origins during the Italian occupation among Libyan poets in exile in Egypt. Writers such as Amid Rafiq and Abdallah Al-Gweiri helped to establish a modern tradition of Libyan literature after the Second World War. The 1960s and early 1970s are regarded as the golden age of Libyan literature: writers such as Sadiq Nauhoum, Khalifa Al-Fakhr, Kamel Hassan Al-Maghur, and Ali Al-Rigaei achieved considerable success. The short story became a popular literary medium in the mid-1960s and the existence of a dozen daily newspapers in a population of fewer than two million indicates the appetite for reading matter in Libya at the time.

After the Revolution the climate changed as Qadhafi and his followers started to clamp down on freedom of expression. In 1974 newspapers were taken into state control, and in 1977 all the publishers and booksellers were merged into one state-owned corporation. Many writers were sent to prison, where most of them remained until 1988. Their treatment mirrors the fate of writers in Eastern Europe during the worst excesses of the communist regimes.

One writer who has fared better than most is Muammar Qadhafi himself, who, in addition to creating his magnum opus, *The Green Book*, has also penned a book of short stories, one of which is entitled "Escape to Hell."

A greatly celebrated Libyan writer these days is Hisham Matar, a Libyan born in New York City, who now lives in Britain. His first novel, *In the Country of Men*, reached the short-list of the UK's prestigious Man Booker Prize in 2006.

SPORTS

Soccer is Libya's leading sport, and it is common to see children, teenagers, or men playing impromptu games on spare patches of ground. Most towns have soccer teams, some up to international standard, which attract crowds of spectators. Many Libyans also avidly follow the progress of European teams.

Basketball is growing in popularity, and with the wealthier sections of society sports such as tennis, bowling, and golf are coming into vogue. These are very much minority sports, but with Libya's ambitious plans to improve tourist facilities, they could attract more players.

SIGHTSEEING

Most people who come to Libya will arrive in Tripoli, one of the most attractive cities in North Africa, and it is well worth setting aside a day or two to have a good look around. The old city (*medina*) is fascinating, with its many *souk*s and ancient mosques. Here you will find the Red

Fort, which houses the Jamahiriya Museum and near to it the arch erected to Marcus Aurelius in 163 CE, one of the few reminders of Roman Tripoli. The Dar Karamanli Museum shows how the well-off lived in the eighteenth century. Modern Tripoli was for the most part

designed and built by the Italians, and offers pleasant walks in tree-lined streets and along the Corniche, which overlooks the harbor.

Visitors to Libya—however short their stay—should not neglect to visit some of the country's World Heritage sites, which are spectacular and relatively uncrowded compared with those on the northern shores of the Mediterranean.

WORLD HERITAGE SITES IN LIBYA

Sabratha

This Roman city lies 40 miles (65 km) west of Tripoli; its easy accessibility makes it popular with Libyans. In Roman times it had a population of 35,000 and a number of magnificent buildings, the ruins of which are still standing. These include the Temple of Isis, the Antonine Temple, the

Basilica of Justinian, the Forum, and the Punic
Mausoleum of Bes (the last dating from pre-
Roman times). The most spectacular feature is the
Theater, restored by the Italians. It has
an 80 foot (25 m) wall behind the stage
incorporating over a hundred Corinthian
columns, and has been used in modern times for
stage performances. The museum has a display of
impressive Roman mosaics.

Leptis Magna

Leptis is 80 miles (125 km) to the east of Tripoli
along the coastal highway. It covers a large area
and is regarded as the most important Roman site
in Libya. In its heyday in the second century CE it
had 80,000 residents and the Roman Emperor

Septimius Severus, who was born in the city, instituted an extensive public building program here using the finest materials from all over the Empire. Among the impressive sights are a Theater that could accommodate 8,000, an Amphitheater, the Severan Forum, the Severan Basilica, the Hadrianic Baths, and the splendid Triumphal Arch of Septimius Severus.

Cyrene and Apollonia

Cyrene (known locally as Shahat) and its port Apollonia (Susa) are just over 125 miles (200 km) to the east of Benghazi. It is the most important Greek city in North Africa in an impressive situation on the slopes of the Jebel Akhdar (Green Mountain). In addition to an Agora and a small Greek Theater, there are

buildings from the Roman period, including a
Forum, the Baths of Trajan, an Amphitheater,
and Temples dedicated to Apollo and Zeus.
The port of Apollonia, established in the seventh
century BCE, just down the hill from Cyrene, is
partially submerged, but retains a number of
interesting buildings, including the Western and
Eastern Basilicas and a Palace. Further
exploration of the scenic Jebel Akhdar will reveal
more ancient sites as well as Ottoman forts.

Ghadames Old Town

Known as the "Pearl of the Desert," this oasis town
close to the Algerian and Tunisian borders is at the
junction of several caravan routes. It is one of the
oldest pre-Saharan cities and an outstanding
example of a traditional settlement. A particular
attraction is the domestic architecture. The houses,

which are built of mud, lime, and palm tree trunks, all intersect. The network of covered alleyways between them, and the attached roofs above, allow passage from one house to another. At roof level there are open-air terraces reserved for the women.

The government has built new houses outside the old town. However, people return to the old center during the summer, as its architecture provides better protection against the heat.

Ghadames represents a triumph of ingenuity in the face of a hostile environment, and is a good place to get to know the friendly people of the desert. It has a lively festival toward the end of the year. There is a regular air service with Tripoli.

Tadrart Acacus Mountains

The rock art paintings of this southwestern corner of Libya date from as long ago as 8,000 BCE and recall a time when the climate of the area was cooler and wetter, allowing a wide range of agricultural activities. Wild animals, such as giraffes, elephants, and antelopes, are pictured in some of the older paintings, while the later ones depict people in chariots believed to be the Garamantes, the ancestors of the Tuareg. The paintings are widely dispersed and the services of a guide are essential. You should allow several days for this trip.

Further Afield

Other places worth visiting if you are staying in Libya for a longer period are Gharian (south of Tripoli) with its pottery and troglodyte houses,

Tobruk with its war cemeteries, and Jaghbub
(south of Tobruk) where the shrine of the
Grand Sanusi is situated.

The Tibesti Mountains in the extreme south
near the border with Chad offer spectacular
desert scenery, but in the past have been out
of bounds to tourists.

culture smart! **libya**

chapter seven

TRAVEL, HEALTH, & SAFETY

BEFORE YOU GO

Libya may be hoping to boost tourism but, unlike other countries in the region, such as Egypt and Tunisia with their highly developed tourist industries, the government gives the impression that it wants to keep foreigners out of the country rather than let them in. Would-be visitors (unless they are Arab or Maltese nationals) still need to obtain entry visas. However, with the ever-present threat from Islamist extremists, there is the likelihood that entry controls will be enforced more strictly on all nationals in future.

To obtain an entry visa you normally need to apply to the Libyan representative in your own country. The visa application process takes a week, but it might be prudent to allow a little longer. As with most official procedures in Libya, this is subject to change. The requirement for an Arabic translation of the details in your passport has, thankfully, now been waived.

If you are traveling to Libya on business you will need to produce an official invitation from a company based in Libya or a Libyan citizen. Tourists who are traveling in a party should follow the advice of the tour company. It is now possible, if you are in a recognized tour group, to have your visa issued at the airport or border crossing of entry on production of an official letter. But you will need to show a copy of this letter to the airline with which you are traveling to Libya, or you will not be allowed on board. The government discourages independent travel, but you can sometimes overcome this problem by obtaining a letter of invitation from a tour company based in Libya.

Holders of Israeli passports are not permitted to enter Libya, and the possession of an Israeli stamp in your passport is sufficient to bar entry.

Foreign nationals with residence permits have greater freedom to move around, but it is important to carry your passport or some other means of identification around with you to show at checkpoints and when entering public buildings.

ARRIVING IN LIBYA
Most people will arrive at Tripoli International Airport and will be required to go through

immigration and customs. Prohibited goods, such as alcohol or drugs, are not allowed into the country and, if found on your person or in your luggage, the penalties are severe.

Arrivals are required to show to customs that they have at least US $500 (or the equivalent) on them. This rule is waived for people traveling with a tour group or who are on official business. Libyan currency may not be imported or exported, and a currency declaration form needs to be completed.

If you are arriving at one of the land borders, procedures can vary. Plenty of time should be allowed as they tend to get very busy.

MONEY

Libya is a country where most transactions are conducted with cash, but there are now some outlets, notably hotels, where credit cards are used. Not so long ago the five star Corinthia Hotel in Tripoli was the only place in Libya that accepted credit cards.

While money can be changed in most of the larger towns along the coast the traveler will find banks are few and far

between in the interior. US dollars are the international currency of choice. Traveler's checks are not accepted. Tripoli now has a few ATMs, but do not rely on finding them in other urban centers. Some hotels are able to change currency, but you cannot rely on it, particularly away from the main cities. So it is advisable always to have plenty of ready cash on you.

TRAVELING AROUND
Driving

The main road is the coastal highway, which runs for more than 1,100 miles (1,800 km) from the Tunisian border to the Egyptian border and is a divided highway for part of the way. In addition there are roads linking most of the main centers, though not all of them are as well maintained as they might be. There are around 38,000 miles (48,000 km) of paved roads and 29,000 miles (36,000 km) of unpaved roadway.

Driving is on the right and seat belts are compulsory. The standard of driving in Libya is poor and care must be exercised at all times, since Libya, which boasts the highest rate of vehicle ownership in Africa, also has one of the highest road accident fatality rates in the world. Libyans tend to be fast drivers—understandable perhaps in view of the great distances that had to be covered when most of the country's aircraft were grounded for want of spare parts and road travel was the only way to get anywhere. Special care must be taken on undivided highways as drivers tend to pass even when traffic is approaching from the opposite direction and have to swerve back into position at the last moment. Traffic circles are particularly hazardous since many drivers fail to slow down at them. Bear in mind that priority is given to vehicles joining the traffic circle, not those on it.

Gasoline is cheap and it is possible to rent cars, although not all are well maintained. You can use your own national driver's license for three months, after which you need to obtain a Libyan license. It is advisable not to let your fuel tank run too low as in some areas filling stations are extremely widely spaced.

In desert areas sand is prone to drifting across the road and drivers may swerve unexpectedly into the middle of the road to avoid the drifts. In rural areas you should also be on the lookout for animals with no road sense crossing the road at random.

Libya's "Marble Arch"
A notable landmark on the coastal highway between Tripoli and Benghazi used to be an imposing arch in the middle of nowhere that was

visible for miles around. British soldiers fighting in the North African campaign of the Second World War nicknamed it "Marble Arch."

The monument was erected by the Italians in the 1930s to celebrate the completion of the coastal highway and as a memorial to the legendary Philaeni brothers from Carthage. According to the legend, Greek Cyrenaica and Punic Carthage decided to fix their border (and thereby avert a war) by dispatching two runners each from Carthage and from Cyrene. The border would be drawn where the runners met. However, the runners from Carthage, who were brothers, managed to run twice the distance that the Cyrene runners ran. The Greeks accused the brothers of cheating and called for the race to be rerun. But the brothers protested their innocence and were even prepared to surrender their lives as proof of their sincerity. The Greeks accepted the offer and killed them. The brothers' graves came to mark the border.

Sadly, "Marble Arch" was dismantled after the 1969 Al-Fateh Revolution, but its remains are displayed on a site next to the roadside (at Medinat Sultan).

Bus Services
There are good bus services, many of them air-conditioned, operating between the main towns.

Another popular form of transportation is the shared taxi, which can sometimes be quicker, albeit less comfortable since the drivers tend to pack in as many people as possible. On some less well-traveled routes taxis are the only means of public transportation.

Air Transportation—International

During the years when sanctions were applied to Libya it was virtually impossible to fly in and out of the country. Visitors had to fly to Tunisia and take the land route into Libya or fly to Malta and take a ferry. Now a number of foreign airlines, such as Air Malta, Alitalia, Austrian, British Airways, Egypt Air, and Tunis Air fly in and out of Tripoli International Airport at Ben Ghasir, 14 miles (24 km) to the south of the city. Jamahiriya Libyan Arab Airlines, a state-owned company, and Afriqiyah, a recently formed private airline based in Libya, also provide international flights. There are far fewer international flights into Benina Airport at Benghazi but an hourly air shuttle service operates between Benghazi and Tripoli.

Air Transportation—Internal

Jamahiriya Libyan Arab Airlines, Buraq Air, and a number of other companies operate flights from Tripoli and Benghazi to airports all over Libya, including Sebha, Al-Beida, Mersa Brega, Misrata, Ghadames, Khufra, and Tobruk. This is the best option where long distances are involved.

When flying from Tripoli you should check whether the plane takes off from Tripoli International Airport or Maatiqa, the former American airbase 2.5 miles (4 km) to the east of the city.

Railways—A Future Possibility

The Italians built a railway to the west of Tripoli, which fell into disuse in the 1960s. Since then the country has had no railway system. That could eventually change, however.

In 1998 plans were drawn up to build, with Chinese assistance, a modern railway along the coast, which would link up with the railway systems of Tunisia and Egypt. Other lines are planned, which should eventually result in a rail network with 1,400 miles (2,257 km) of 1.435 meter gauge track. It was hoped to have the first trains running in 2008, but like many projects in Libya it is beset with uncertainty and delay.

Sea Transportation

At one time, when the air embargo was in force, there was a nightly ferry service between Malta and Tripoli but nowadays the ferry no longer operates on a regular basis. Cruise ships occasionally dock in Tripoli and other ports.

WHERE TO STAY

Compared with other countries in North Africa, which handle large numbers of tourists, the

hospitality industry is relatively undeveloped. Hotels are geared to the business traveler rather than the tourist and their quality tends not to match their high prices. That is likely to change over the next few years, though, if Libya implements its ambitious plans to develop tourism.

Libya's most modern and luxurious hotel is the twenty-six-story Corinthia Bab Europa in Tripoli, which opened in 2003. There are plans for more hotels of this standard and several resort developments along Libya's attractive Mediterranean coast are also underway. If you have to make your own accommodation arrangements it is advisable to reserve in advance. This is particularly necessary in the case of hotels close to the main tourist sites, which are often fully reserved by tour groups. In Tripoli prior reservation is essential during the period of the Tripoli International Fair and some of the other major trade fairs that take place there.

Sabratha or Leptis Magna do not present a problem as it is possible to make a day excursion to either of these, but if you are planning to visit Cyrene you really need to find accommodation close by, either in Beida or, better still, Apollonia. For the budget traveler youth hostels are worth investigation; you do not need to possess a membership card from your own national Youth Hostels Association to stay at these.

Bear in mind that it is against the law in Libya for unmarried couples to share a room, and some hotels may insist on proof of marriage before allocating a room to a couple.

HEALTH

Unlike sub-Saharan Africa Libya is a fairly salubrious place to live, with no incidence of malaria, yellow fever, cholera, or smallpox. There are pharmacies and health centers in all the major towns, but it is advisable to bring certain items with you, such as antiseptic ointment, foot powder, prickly heat powder, insect repellent, motion sickness tablets, aspirin or the equivalent, sunscreen, antidiarrheal pills, and adhesive strips.

If you take reasonable precautions, you should stay fit and healthy. Take care about what you eat and drink, just to be on the safe side. It is better to opt for bottled drinks (including water) and, at roadside restaurants, cooked food rather than cold dishes and salads. On hot sunny days a hat should be worn to avoid heatstroke, and when traveling in the desert it is important to avoid becoming dehydrated by drinking plenty of water.

HIV exists in Libya, though not in the epidemic proportions found south of the Sahara, and hepatitis is common among immigrant workers from sub-Saharan countries. While vaccinations against hepatitis A, polio, and typhoid are recommended, they are not mandatory.

Libya boasts reasonably good health-care facilities, and many of its doctors have been trained in Europe. However, not all speak good English. Tripoli has both private and public health clinics, and there are health-care facilities in all the major towns. If you fall seriously ill, evacuation to Tunisia or Malta may well be preferable. As a precaution you should take out private medical insurance to cover the duration of your stay.

SAFETY

In 2004 the insurance broker Aon rated Libya and Greenland as the safest countries for travel. While there are some places that are best avoided—notably the city of Sebha in the Fezzan, which has a reputation for lawlessness—generally speaking, Libyans are law-abiding and there is little violent crime in the country. Thieves and pickpockets exist, especially in crowded places such as markets, so it is not a good idea to carry valuables around with you. If you are unfortunate enough to be robbed, you should inform the police and contact your national consulate in Tripoli.

Libya takes the threat of terrorism very seriously and you may find that you have to go through security checks in public buildings and even some hotels.

The authorities place restrictions on travel—especially in the interior and the border areas—

apart from the official land border crossings with Egypt and Tunisia. For travel in the desert you will need to obtain prior permission and may be obliged to take a police guard with you.

In the larger towns and cities you may come across gatherings of people remonstrating vociferously. It could be some kind of a political demonstration—which may or may not have been sanctioned by the government. But if it isn't official, you don't want to get injured or arrested when the police or army swoop down. Equally, it could be a relatively harmless occurrence, such as a party or high jinks before or after a sports match. Whatever it is, it best to exercise prudence and get out of the way.

If you are a woman you will be perfectly safe, but it is advisable not to wander around on your own and draw attention to yourself by exposing too much flesh or by staring at people. It is more sensible to go out in a group or with a male escort. Fortunately, you are less likely to be pestered by young males than in other parts of North Africa.

PHOTOGRAPHY, AND OTHER ADVICE
While you are perfectly free to photograph or video tourist sites, you should exercise discretion elsewhere. Not everyone will take

kindly to being photographed in the street or other public places, and if you are invited to a party or meal you should first of all ask permission to take pictures.

Photographing airports, military installations, police stations, checkpoints and border crossings, industrial complexes, oil refineries, and government buildings is strictly forbidden. There are security personnel everywhere, and if caught you could find yourself under arrest.

Libyans can be sensitive about non-Muslims entering mosques and may bar you. If you wish to see inside a mosque—even if it is a famous one mentioned in a tourist guide—go at a quiet time of day and ask the permission of whomever is in charge. Make sure you are dressed appropriately and do not photograph anyone at prayer.

People are permitted to practice their own faith in Libya and there are a number of Christian churches operating in the country (including Roman Catholic and Anglican/Episcopalian). Non-Muslims are not permitted to proselytize, however, so missionary work is definitely out of the question.

chapter eight

BUSINESS BRIEFING

THE BUSINESS CLIMATE

There has never been a better time to do business in Libya. After more than three decades of isolation the country is starting to open up to outside investors in order to stimulate the economy.

Its oil industry is a particularly attractive prospect. Having set the target of increasing oil production from the present 1.2 million barrels a day to 3 million barrels a day, it is in need of investment and foreign expertise. With this in mind the government has issued new drilling concessions to foreign firms from the USA, Russia, China, and other countries.

Modern equipment is needed to exploit both the older oil fields and new finds more efficiently. While sanctions were in force, Libya was unable to import the necessary technology and spare parts to maintain its output. The transportation infrastructure also deteriorated.

The country will have no difficulty in finding a market for any extra oil it produces, since it is of good quality with low sulfur content, and its oil terminals are in easy reach of European markets. With an estimated 2 percent of global oil reserves, oil holds the key to Libya's prosperity for many years to come.

Petroleum is far and away the country's main export. The country also boasts a petrochemical industry and exports 140,000 barrels a day of petroleum products as well as natural gas, much of it to Italy. It also has indigenous aluminum, and iron and steel industries. Agriculture is geared to local consumption rather than the export trade and a large proportion of food is imported.

There are also considerable opportunities for companies involved in construction, ports, education and training, health care, transport and logistics, and power generation. The country's civil airports need a makeover, there are plans for eleven desalination plants to supplement the water provided by the Great Man-Made River (see page 53), and the Libyans are building a nuclear power plant with American assistance.

The government is also keen to build up its tourist industry with the aim of attracting one million tourists annually by 2015. This may sound ambitious considering that visitors totaled a modest 130,000 in 2006, and as yet there is insufficient infrastructure in place to deal with increased numbers. But there are ambitious plans to develop a resort on and around Farwa Island near the Tunisian border, with further resorts planned close to Tobruk and Leptis Magna.

POTENTIAL PITFALLS

Foreign Investment Law No. 5 passed in 1997, with its subsequent amendments and implementing regulations, offers considerable scope for potential investors. It allows 100 percent foreign equity ownership for licensed companies, five years' exemption from corporate income tax (with a possible three-year extension if net profits are reinvested), exemption from customs duties in the early years of a project, permission to repatriate profits and employ expatriates, and also to own and lease property.

Although such favorable business terms must gladden the heart of even the most hard-bitten investor, there are a number of potential pitfalls of which one needs to be aware. A major problem is that in most sectors—the oil business is the honorable exception—Libya lacks a proper business infrastructure.

It can take an age to arrive at an agreement that is acceptable to all parties, and even then would-be investors should not assume that everything is cut and dried. Government intervention can sometimes overturn plans, as was the case with an Italian company that signed a concession to develop Farwa Island, only to find the project shelved in favor of another scheme.

Licensing involves a protracted approval process and the law lacks clarity on a number of matters, such as the minimum capital required for a project. No guidance is given as to the requirements for gaining approval, and foreign investors can find themselves disadvantaged when competing against state enterprises. In the event of a dispute it is not possible to seek redress in a foreign court. While the Foreign Investment Law has many good points, it contradicts much of the old legislation that abolished commercial companies and private property rights. The law may have changed, but it will take time for the arbitrary practices and lengthy consultation processes that were developed during the Revolutionary period to be eradicated completely.

PERSONAL RELATIONSHIPS ARE VITAL

Libyans can be canny business people who appreciate a good deal when they see one. They prefer to do business, though, with people they have got to know and trust rather than with strangers who show complete ignorance of their culture and traditions, who are here today and gone tomorrow. So be prepared for the long haul.

This is a country where personal relationships count and help to offset the weak formal and legal structures under which business has had to operate in the past. The first priority is to establish trust with a potential partner or customer, and this calls for flexibility and patience. Do not expect to have everything wrapped up at the end of one meeting or even one visit. It may take a number of visits before an agreement is reached. The good news is that, once you have established a good working relationship with a person or firm, things become much easier and smoother.

It is therefore essential to do your homework before you arrive for any meeting, and not limit your horizons to knowledge of the goods or services you are selling. Cultivate the art of small talk and ensure that you are well informed about Libyan customs and traditions and also the organizations and people you will be dealing with.

My Word Is My Bond

Some time ago the British Council, a UK cultural organization, recruited lecturers and teachers for Libya and guaranteed their contracts. However, they were concerned that one of their English lecturers had not been issued with a contract by the University. He took the matter up with the Dean of the Faculty where he was teaching.

The Dean was surprised by the Council's concern since he considered a verbal agreement to be sufficient, whereas a written contract was hardly worth the paper it was written on.

While in modern business written contracts are unavoidable, Libyans still tend to place more faith in verbal agreements and a handshake than the written word.

BUSINESS ETIQUETTE

Business hours vary according to the time of year. In the winter they tend to be between 8:00 a.m. and 1:00 p.m. and between 4:00 p.m. and 6.30 pm. In summer they are from 7:00 a.m. to 2:00 p.m. If you have a choice in the matter, it is best to avoid making a business visit during the holy month of Ramadan when tempers can get frayed. If a visit at this time is unavoidable, try to schedule your appointments for the morning, the earlier the better. Libyans expect their visitors to be punctual, even if they are not scrupulously so themselves. You should therefore be prepared for delays and avoid planning a tight schedule for yourself. You don't want to find yourself in the embarrassing position of having to dash off to another appointment just as you reach a crucial stage in your current meeting, which would be disrespectful to your host.

Libyans also expect people to be tactful and courteous. It is not acceptable to criticize people directly or to try to force an issue, as Libyans dislike confrontation. They often shy away from making instant decisions, possibly because they are aware that any plan they agree to could be countermanded from on high. (Fortunately, the oil industry is relatively immune from outside interference.) If a person appears evasive about one of your suggestions, it is better not to press the matter but to change tack.

You should dress formally, even if the weather is hot, unless specifically told not to. So men should avoid shorts and open necked shirts, while women need to make sure that their arms are covered and not too much leg is revealed. Dressing casually for a business meeting could be interpreted as a sign of disrespect, and Libyans—like most Arabs—expect to be treated with respect and dignity.

THE LANGUAGE OF BUSINESS

Many business people and officials speak English, but some who feel their English is not good enough may wish to conduct business using an interpreter, usually a more junior member of staff. If your knowledge of Arabic is sketchy or nonexistent, it would be sensible to take an Arabic speaker along with you as your interpreter, just to ensure that there are no misunderstandings.

Although English is gaining currency as Libya's second language, it does not have the same official status it enjoys in other Arab countries and many African ones, and you should bear in mind that contracts and agreements have to be in Arabic. Business cards are an essential tool in your armory and it is sensible to have your details in English on one side and Arabic on the reverse. Ideally, your sales literature should also be in Arabic.

DEALING WITH THE GOVERNMENT

Because of large scale nationalization of the Libyan economy after the Revolution the distinction between civil servant and company employee does not really apply. Many of the larger companies, including banks and insurance companies, are either government owned or are run by government appointees.

As in many places in the Arab world, the wheels of government grind slowly, and you may get frustrated by the bureaucratic obstacles you encounter. Libya has an extensive bureaucracy, and it is estimated that around 70 percent of the workforce are employed directly or indirectly by the government. Most Libyans want to work in the public sector because it offers them security and influence, even if the pay is low.

However, as already mentioned, the oil sector is by far the most efficient part of the government and employs some very bright and motivated people. Higher education, too, has many forward-looking people in its ranks. But some areas of government are less well organized, and it is sometimes difficult to find people who are ready to make decisions.

FIRST APPROACHES

Cold calling seldom yields satisfactory results in the West, and is even less likely to in Arab countries such as Libya. To smooth the way foreign businesspeople need to enlist partners or agents who have in-depth knowledge of the Libyan market, and it is particularly important to find someone to steer you through the legal labyrinth.

You need all the help and support you can get in what can seem to a newcomer like a very alien environment, and if your country has an embassy in Libya —most do nowadays—this should be your first port of call. Be prepared to interrogate the commercial attaché, whose job is to keep aware of and monitor business opportunities.

Wasta—the practice of having a network of influential friends and relations who can exert influence—is still well engrained in the Arab world, and if you know the brother or cousin of an influential businessman or government official this can often smooth your way to an appointment with the great man himself. If not, the process may take longer, and you will need to call on the services of your embassy. The initial meeting will probably be a "getting to know you" affair, and provided you make a good impression should lead to several more.

MEETINGS

Meetings can be protracted affairs and it can take time before you get down to the nitty-gritty of the business discussion. Expect to start off with a cup of coffee or tea, or both, and an exchange of pleasantries. You may be asked how you are enjoying Libya, about your job, your family, your hobbies, rather than the real purpose of your visit.

If you are a novice in the Middle East, you may think this is a waste of time and feel you have to steer the conversation around to the business matters that you are here to discuss. As we have already seen, however, Libyans do not compartmentalize their lives into work and leisure in the same way as many Westerners do, and they approach meetings from a very different viewpoint.

A Libyan businessman is as interested in you as he is in the product or service you have come to sell. A meeting, particularly an initial encounter, is important because it offers a chance for him (rarely a her) to size you up and decide whether you are the kind of person he wishes to do business with. When the time is right—and perhaps when you are least expecting it—the discussion will suddenly turn to business matters. You may be asked to give a presentation there and then, so it is always sensible to carry a laptop around with you. Expect interruptions during your presentation and don't be offended if you are cut short in mid-flight.

Many Libyans just want to get the gist of the service or product on offer rather than be given detailed explanations.

One irritation for some Western businessmen is that they arrive expecting to have a private meeting with a business leader or a department head plus one or two of his advisers. On arrival, though, they find a number of other people in the office at the same time who have turned up to see the man in charge for all manner of reasons.

This tradition is reminiscent of medieval courts in Europe. The monarch sat in state and people approached him with petitions, problems they expected him to solve, contracts to be signed, matters requiring a decision. In a similar fashion a Libyan executive or department head often has to juggle a number of different matters and people at once. Delegation is not well developed in Libya and every person on the staff has the right to see the person at the top of the hierarchy.

Of course, you will come across Libyans educated abroad who will prefer to conduct meetings in a more disciplined way. The technocrats of the oil industry are for the most part exemplary in their dealings with foreign firms. However, the traditional way of doing things is still very much entrenched and you have a better chance of success if you are prepared to be flexible and learn to "go with the flow."

Libyans, like all Arabs, are hospitable people and may insist on taking you out for a meal. This should be regarded as an opportunity to develop personal relationships further rather than to discuss business matters. However, as indicated already, because work and leisure are not necessarily separate in the Libyan mind, business could figure prominently.

THE ART OF NEGOTIATION

It is difficult to lay down hard and fast rules on the best was to conduct negotiations, and newcomers to Libya would be best advised to rely on local business and legal advisers. As has been emphasized many times in this book, first of all you need to build up trust, and it is only after this has been achieved that you can hope to build a satisfactory business relationship.

A crucial question: should you, as a bargaining ploy, quote a higher price than you expect to receive for the product or service you are offering? Again, you need to rely on your local advisers. You also need to bear in mind that a number of companies from around the world are eager to gain a foothold in the Libyan market, and firms from China and Korea offer very competitive deals. It is probably a better plan to persuade customers of the quality and uniqueness of what you have on offer.

Remember to show courtesy at all times. Libyans like to be treated with respect, whatever their position in the hierarchy of the business or government, and you should never talk down to them.

Finally you should regard negotiations as ongoing, and make an effort to keep the relationship fresh by regular visits and meetings. If you go away once the deal is done and fail to return, you may be forgotten, allowing others to jump in and take your business.

WOMEN IN BUSINESS

Although a woman's place has traditionally been in the home, Libyan women are starting to make their mark in business and the professions. Some are attaining senior positions in the judiciary.

If you find that you are meeting with a female executive, do not think that you will have a less than challenging time. Modern Libyan women are well educated—on average they have spent longer in education than men—and they can be astute negotiators.

If you are a businessman, there are certain caveats to observe when dealing with a Libyan woman in business. You must ensure that you keep your relationship strictly on a professional basis. You will only cause embarrassment if you ask a Libyan woman out to dinner or a night on the town. In the unlikely circumstance that she does accept, she will probably bring along a chaperone—her husband or big brother. However, if she makes an offer of hospitality (which will be an appropriate one), it should be accepted without hesitation.

Do not be overly friendly. Don't insist on shaking hands, but if she offers you her hand you should take it. Don't ask personal questions but confine your conversation to business and professional matters.

A Western businesswoman in Libya may find she has the best of both worlds. Men will treat you as an *azuz*, like an older woman with status who inspires respect and even awe. Libyan women executives will relate more readily to you than they would to a male. They are more likely to talk about personal matters with you and invite you into their homes to meet the female members of their family.

chapter nine

COMMUNICATING

THE IMPORTANCE OF ARABIC

The official language of Libya is Arabic, and anyone planning to visit or stay in Libya for any length of time would be well advised to ensure they have at least a smattering of the language. Fortunately, many Libyans are conversant in English, Italian or (in the south of Libya) French, but standards vary. Qadhafi's Arabicization policy after the 1969 Revolution meant that the teaching of foreign languages was given a low priority in schools and universities, and at one stage in the 1980s English teaching was banned altogether. Road signs, shop names, and posters that were once bilingual—as they still are in most other parts of the Arab world—came to be written only in Arabic characters. For visitors who do not read Arabic this can cause problems.

Spoken Arabic

Arabic, which is a Semitic language, is the mother tongue of around 220 million people in the

Middle East and North Africa, from Morocco in the West to Oman in the East. Its use spread throughout the region—and even into Spain—with the Arab conquests and the propagation of Islam. There is, however, considerable variation in the colloquial language both between countries and within countries.

As we have seen, Libya has three distinct dialect groups corresponding to the historic regions of the country. Arabic speakers from the Levant and the Gulf admit to having initial difficulties in understanding the dialect spoken in Tripolitania, but Libyans have few problems in understanding Egyptian or Lebanese Arabic because of exposure to films and other media emanating from these countries.

Written Arabic

There are two main types of written Arabic: Classical Arabic, the language of the Qur'an and classical literature; and Modern Standard Arabic, the language of the media and the form in which most letters and official documents are written.

Visitors, whether on short or long stays, will find a little knowledge of written Arabic of tremendous benefit, if only to find their way around. All signs written in Roman script disappeared soon after the Revolution of 1969 and some recent European visitors to Libya have confessed to feeling disoriented as a consequence. Words are written from right to left and many of the letters are connected.

Arabic words are generally formed from three consonant roots. For instance, *k*, *t*, and *b* give rise to the words *KaTaBa*—to write; *KiTaB*—book; *KuTuBi*—bookseller; *KaTiB*—secretary; *maKTaB*—office; *maKTaBa*—library, and so on.

THE ARABIC ALPHABET

The Arabic script evolved from Aramaic, a language used widely in the Middle East in ancient times, and its earliest recorded use is in an inscription that dates from 512 CE. The alphabet, shown opposite, consists of twenty-eight characters, of which three are long vowels. Note that certain characters are differentiated by the number of dots above or below them.

The form of many characters changes according to its position in the word—initial, medial, or final—or whether it stands alone:

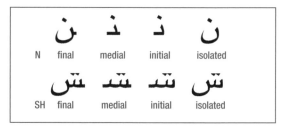

The Arabic Alphabet

ا	alif	*the long vowel aa*	ض	daad	*d (emphatic d)*
ب	baa	*b*	ط	ta	*t (emphatic t)*
ت	taa	*t*	ظ	dhaal	*dh (emphatic dh)*
ث	thaa	*th (soft English th)*	ع	ayn	*'ayn (glottal as in "uh-oh")*
ج	jeem	*dj (soft, as in genre)*	غ	ghayn	*r, gh (strong uvular r like German)*
ح	ha	*ha (heavily aspirated h sound)*	ف	feh	*f*
خ	kha	*kh (like Spanish jota)*	ق	qaaf	*q*
د	daal	*d*	ك	kaaf	*k*
ذ	dhal	*dh (hard English th)*	ل	laam	*l*
ر	ra	*r (rolled r)*	م	meem	*m*
ز	zain	*z*	ن	noon	*n*
س	seen	*s*	ه	ha	*h (breathy h)*
ش	sheen	*sh*	و	waaw	*w, oo*
ص	saad	*s (emphatic s)*	ي	yaaw	*y, ee*

In addition to these characters there are three short vowels (/a/, /i/, and /u/), which are pronounced but seldom written down. They appear in the Qur'an and other classical texts and some schoolbooks. Each vowel is placed above the consonant that precedes it. A small o signifies that no vowel follows.

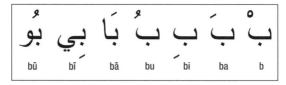

Arabic words are written from right to left. Numbers, however, are written from left to right, and you should note that what we in the West refer to as Arabic numbers are different from those in use in Libya and most other countries in the Arab world.

How Do You Spell Qadhafi?

There is no generally accepted authority for writing Arabic words or names in Roman script, and certain consonants in Arabic that have no exact equivalent in English are a particular problem. It is said that the name of Libya's leader can be spelled in thirty-two different ways. Here are some of them: Gadafi, Gadafy. Gaddafi, Ghaddafi, Ghaddafy, Gheddafi, Kadafi, Kaddafi, Kadhafi, Kazzafi, Khadaffi, Khadafi, Khaddafi, Qadafi, Qaddafi, Qadhafi, Qatafi, Quathafi, and Qudhafi.

His first name admits similar variations, including Moamar, Moamer, Moammar, Mo'ammar, Mohammer, Mu'ammar, Muamar, Mu'amar, Muammar, and Mu'ammar.

The definite article usually precedes the surname in written Arabic (as in Al-Qadhafi), but when the name is romanized it may be dropped.

OTHER LANGUAGES OF LIBYA

Of the Berber languages the most widely used is Nafusi, which is spoken in the area around Nalut, Jefren, and the coastal area of Zuara west of Tripoli. Tuareg is spoken in the oases around Ghat, and the Ghadames dialect in the oasis of that name. The Eastern Berber language of Sokna is spoken in the Tripolitanian oasis of that name and in Awjilah in Cyrenaica, but appears to be facing extinction. There is also an Indo-European language called Domari (also known as Nawari), which is related to Romani and Eastern Punjabi and is estimated to have 30,000 speakers in the south of Libya.

FACE-TO-FACE

Communication is not confined to speaking and writing. Body language can be just as crucial as the spoken word. Here are a few suggestions that should enable you to communicate effectively and make a favorable impression.

DOS AND DON'TS

- Look people in the eye when speaking.
- Be respectful, diplomatic, and courteous.
- Use your right hand when giving and eating.
- Avoid getting into an argument.
- Use a person's correct title.
- Take off your shoes when entering a Libyan home.
- Express yourself clearly to avoid misunderstandings.
- Confine your conversation to noncontroversial topics.
- Don't display the soles of your feet.
- Don't back away if someone comes too close to you.
- Don't discuss Libyan politics.
- Don't try to be too direct or forward.
- Don't make disparaging remarks about Islam.
- Don't turn your back on anyone.
- Don't be blunt or sarcastic.
- Don't make comments that could be misinterpreted.

THE MEDIA

There are around 1.5 million radios and 750,000 televisions in use in Libya. As we have seen, most Libyan broadcast media are state controlled and have limited appeal, but a private radio and TV station, Allibya, has opened recently. Many Libyans prefer to tune in to foreign TV stations and satellite broadcasts. News programs in French and English are broadcast in the evening.

In addition to more than a dozen Arabic newspapers that are government controlled, there is a biweekly English newspaper, *The Tripoli Post*. Foreign publications were not readily available as this book went to print, but Qadhafi's son, Saif Al-Islam, is believed to have plans to distribute foreign titles in the future.

TELECOMMUNICATIONS

The telecommunications system is undergoing modernization. A mobile cellular system became operational in 1996 and there are an estimated 250,000 cell phones in use. Among the providers are Al Madar (linked to Vodaphone), Libyana, and Thuraya. There are roughly 750,000 fixed line telephones. The country code for Libya is 218.

There are estimated to be more than 200,000 Internet users and the country has four Internet service providers in addition to the state-owned General Post and Telecommunications Co. Internet cafés exist in several towns and are popular with the young. The Internet country code is .ly. The postal service is reasonably reliable.

CONCLUSION

Half a century has passed since oil was discovered in Libya—giving a much needed boost to an underdeveloped, impoverished country. A great deal has been achieved since then, though not without pain and disruption to people's lives. On the positive side, Libya is a more egalitarian society than most in the area, is reasonably stable, and offers excellent business opportunities for those prepared to seek them out.

Yet there are drawbacks. Many first-time visitors find Libya inefficient, disorganized, and bureaucratic. They perceive the Libyans themselves to be arrogant, offhanded, prickly, proud, uncommunicative, uncooperative, and unsophisticated compared with other Arabs. But if you probe more deeply, you will find such attitudes just a front, a means whereby

Libyans protect themselves against the hostile world and unwelcome strangers.

Those who persist, who get to know the history, culture, and traditions of Libya, will see an entirely different picture. Once trust has been established they discover that basically the Libyans are delightful people, laid-back and friendly, who are also kind and generous. Respect their traditions, take an interest, and behave in a civilized manner in their country, and they will treat you as an honored guest.

Appendix 1: Understanding Signs in Arabic

Here are some signs that you will come across as you travel around Libya. Try to match the letters of the alphabet with the Arabic words below.

Apollonia (Susa)	سوسة
Beida (Al-Beida)	البيضاء
Benghazi	بنغازي
Cyrene (Shahat)	شحات
Derna	درنة
Ghadames	غدامس
Gharian	غريان
Khoms (Al-Khoms)	الخمس
Leptis Magna (Libda)	لبدة
Libya	ليبيا
Misrata	مصراتة
Sabratha	صبراتة
Sebha	سبها
Sirt	سرت
Tobruk	طبرق
Tripoli (Trabulus)	طرابلس
Zuara	زوارة
bank (*masraf*)	مصرف
hotel (*funduq*)	فندق
restaurant (*mat'am*)	مطعم
square (*meidan*)	ميدان
street (*shar'a*)	شارع
town center (*merkuz al medina*)	مركز المدينة

Appendix 2: Useful Arabic Words and Phrases

Greetings

Like all Arabs, Libyans appreciate foreigners who make attempts to speak their language—even if it does not extend much beyond greetings. Men greet each other with a handshake and may kiss each other on both cheeks. But kissing a person of the opposite sex, if not a close relative, is frowned on.

Salaam Aleikum

A conversation normally begins with *Salaam aleikum* (Peace be upon you).This will generally elicit the response *Aleikum salam.*

Sabah Alkheer

Alternatively you can refer to the time of day: *Sabah Alkheer* (Good Morning) or *Masa Alkheer* (Good Afternoon/Evening).

Ahlan wa Sahlan

If a person has come to see you, you can put him or her at ease with the words *Ahlan wa Sahlan* (Welcome).

Keef Halak?

Keef Halak? (How are you?) requires the response *bahee* or *tayib, alhemdulilah* (Fine, thanks be to God). Note that the phrase *Alhemdulilah* occurs frequently in conversation and often supplants the word "yes."

In sha Allah

Another common phrase is *In sha Allah* (God willing). This is often used in relation to future events and plans, and while generally signifying assent does leave room for a certain ambiguity: "perhaps" rather than a definite "yes." When taking leave of someone, it is traditional to say *Ma Salama* (Peace be with you).

Other Common Expressions

aywa or *na'am* yes

la no

min fadlak please

shukran thank you

mabrouk congratulations

shi ismak what's your name?

ismi John my name is John

wain where?

ma lish "it doesn't matter" or "don't worry" or "don't get worked up" (depending on the circumstances). This typifies the Libyans' laid-back approach to life.

bukra "tomorrow," like the Spanish "manana." Another example of this. Why do today what you can put off till tomorrow?

ma feesh "we haven't any" or "there is none." This is heard regularly. *Fee* means there is.

Words to Use at the Market

giddash? how much?

ghalee expensive

ghalee halba too expensive

rakhees cheap

jameel beautiful

jadeed new

qadeem old

kabeer big

sagheer small

mumtaz excellent

shwaya a little

Numbers
1 *wahid*
2 *itneen*
3 *talata*
4 *arb'a*
5 *khamsa*
6 *sitta*
7 *sab'a*
8 *tamanya*
9 *tissa'*
10 *ashra*
11 *idash*
12 *itnash*
20 *ishreen*
21 *wahid wa ishreen* (one and twenty)
30 *talateen*
100 *miyya*
200 *myaatein*
300 *talata miyya*
1,000 *alf*
2,000 *alfein*
3,000 *talat alf*

Days of the Week
Sunday *yoom al ahad* (first day)
Monday *yoom al itneen*
Tuesday *yoom al talata*
Wednesday *yoom al arba'a*
Thursday *yoom al khamees*
Friday *yoom al juma'*
Saturday *yoom as sabt*

Appendix 3: Libyan Poetry

Poetry is one of Libya's longest traditions. One of Libya's best-known poems was written by Sheikh Rajib Buhwaish Al-Manfi. It describes the suffering and despair felt by the thousands of Libyans who were forced into concentration camps set up by Italy between 1929 and 1931. The following excerpts are taken from an English translation.

My only illness is being at al Agailla camp, the imprisonment of my tribe and the long way from home . . .

My only illness is the loss of my beloved, good-looking strong people on top of camels and best-looking horses . . .

My only illness is having to lose my dignity at my advanced age and the loss of our finest people, the ones we cannot do without . . .

My only illness is the torturing of our young women, with their bodies exposed . . .

My only illness is the loss of sweet and good people and having to be ruled by grotesque people whose straight faces show nothing but misery . . .

My only illness is the broken hearts, the falling tears and all the herds with no protector or care-taker . . .

Further Reading

Azema, James, *Libya Handbook*, Bath: Footprint Handbooks, 2000.

Bradley, Chris, *Pocket Guide to Libya*, London: Berlitz, 2006.

Di Vita Antonia and Robert Polidori, *Libya: The Lost Cities of the Roman Empire*, Cologne: Konemann Verlag, 1999. ADD UMLAUT OVER O

Ham, Anthony. *Libya*. Melbourne: Lonely Planet, 2007.

Matar, Hisham, *In the Country of Men*, London: Penguin Books, 2006.

Qadhafi, Muammar, *Escape to Hell and Other Stories*, London: John Blake Publishing, 1999.

Qadhafi, Muammar and Edmond Jouve, *My Vision*, London: John Blake Publishing, 2005.

Vandewalle, Dirk, *A History of Modern Libya*, Cambridge: Cambridge University Press, 2006.

Williams, Gwyn, *Green Mountain*, London: Faber, 1968.

Arabic

Complete Arabic: The Basics. New York: Living Langue, 2005.

In-Flight Arabic. New York: Living Language, 2001.

Dickinson, Eerick, *Spoken Libyan Arabic*, Springfield, Illinois: Dunwoody Press, 2004.

Useful Web Sites

www.libyana.org
www.libya-watona.com
www.libyaonline.com
www.libyalinks.com
www.libyadaily.com
www.araboo.com

culture smart! libya

Index